The Ultimate Keto Diet

Cookbook for Beginners

1600 Quick, Low-Carb and Delicious Keto Recipes for Weight Loss and Healthy Living, Includes 4 Weeks Meal Plan

Esther Frost

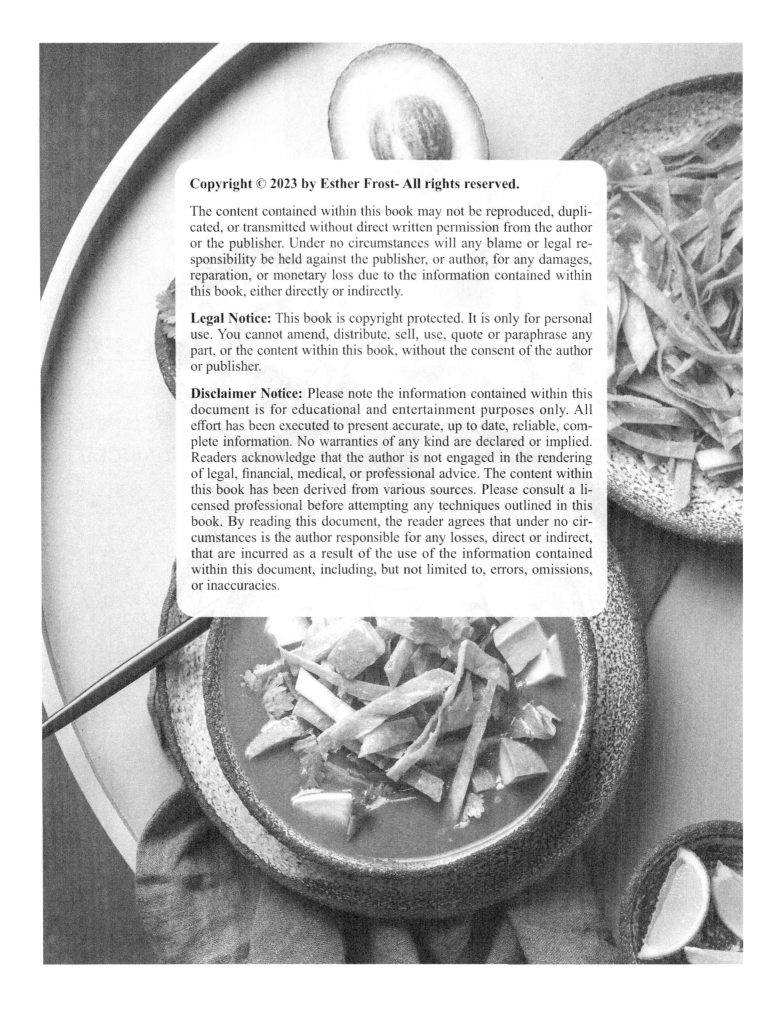

CONTENTS

Pork, Beef & Lamb Recipes

Fish And Seafood Recipes

Vegan, Vegetable & Meatless Recipes 61

Desserts And Drinks 74

INTRODUCTION

Hello everyone, my name is Esther Frost and I am excited to introduce you to my latest project, the "1600 Days Recipes Keto Diet Cookbook for Beginners". As someone who has been passionate about health and wellness for many years, I am thrilled to share my knowledge and experience with others through this guide.

I have always been interested in developing healthy eating habits and maintaining an active lifestyle. Over the years, I have tried various diets and approaches to healthy living, but I found that the ketogenic diet provided the most noticeable and sustainable results. Not only did I lose weight, but I also experienced a boost in energy and mental clarity.

However, I found that sticking to a keto diet can be challenging, especially for beginners. I noticed that many people struggled to come up with meal ideas that were both delicious and compliant with the keto guidelines. That's when I decided to create this cookbook, to provide a comprehensive resource for those who are interested in starting a keto diet but don't know where to begin.

This cookbook contains 1600 days' worth of recipes that are simple, delicious and easy to prepare. The recipes are designed to help beginners transition to a keto diet smoothly and to help them stick to the diet in the long run. The book is divided into different sections, which include breakfast, lunch, dinner, snacks, and desserts. Each recipe comes with clear instructions and nutritional information.

In addition to the recipes, the book also includes an introduction to the keto diet, its benefits, and potential side effects. I also share some tips on how to successfully follow a keto diet, including how to stock your pantry, how to meal plan, and how to eat out while staying keto-friendly.

Overall, I am confident that the "1600 Days Recipes Keto Diet Cookbook for Beginners" will be a valuable resource for anyone who is interested in starting a keto diet or who is looking for new keto meal ideas. Whether you are a seasoned keto dieter or just starting out, this cookbook will provide you with the tools and inspiration you need to succeed. Thank you for considering my cookbook, and I hope it brings you as much joy and success as it has brought me.

Are you ready?

Let's dive right into it.

What Exactly is The Keto Diet?

The ketogenic, or keto, diet is a low-carbohydrate, high-fat diet that has gained popularity in recent years due to its potential health benefits. The diet is based on the concept of ketosis, which is a metabolic state in which the body burns fat for fuel instead of carbohydrates.

The traditional Western diet is high in carbohydrates, which are broken down into glucose and used as the body's primary source of energy. However, when carbohydrates are limited, the body is forced to find an alternative fuel source. In the absence of glucose, the liver converts fat into molecules called ketone bodies, which are then used as fuel by the body.

The keto diet typically consists of 70-80% fat, 10-20% protein, and 5-10% carbohydrates. The goal is to reduce carbohydrate intake to a level low enough to induce ketosis, typically around 20-50 grams per day.

Foods that are commonly consumed on a keto diet include meat, fish, eggs, dairy products, nuts, seeds, and low-carbohydrate vegetables such as spinach and broccoli. Foods that are high in carbohydrates, such as bread, pasta, rice, and sugary snacks, are strictly limited.

There are several potential health benefits associated with the keto diet. One of the most well-known benefits is weight loss. By reducing carbohydrate intake and increasing fat consumption, the body is forced to burn stored fat for energy, resulting in weight loss. The diet may also improve blood sugar control, reduce inflammation, and improve cardiovascular health markers such as blood pressure and cholesterol levels.

However, the keto diet is not without potential risks and side effects. Some people may experience the "keto flu" during the initial stages of the diet, which can cause symptoms such as fatigue, headaches, and nausea. The diet may also be difficult to sustain in the long term and may lead to nutrient deficiencies if not carefully planned.

Overall, the keto diet is a low-carbohydrate, high-fat diet that has gained popularity in recent years due to its potential health benefits. While it may not be suitable for everyone, it can be a viable option for those looking to lose weight, improve their health, and optimize their metabolic function.

What is The Difference Between A Low-carb Diet and A Keto Diet?

Both low-carb diets and the keto diet involve restricting carbohydrate intake, but there are several key differences between them.

1.Macronutrient Ratios
The most significant difference between low-carb diets and the keto diet is the macronutrient ratio. Low-carb diets typically involve reducing carbohydrate intake to around 100-150 grams per day, while the keto diet requires reducing carbohydrate intake to around 20-50 grams per day. In contrast, low-carb diets tend to have a higher proportion of protein and moderate fat intake, while the keto diet is characterized by high fat intake, moderate protein intake, and very low carbohydrate intake.

2.Ketosis
The keto diet is designed to induce a state of ketosis, in which the body burns fat for fuel instead of carbohydrates. By limiting carbohydrate intake to a very low level, the body is forced to produce ketones from fat stores, which can be used as an alternative fuel source. Low-carb diets do not necessarily aim to induce ketosis, although some individuals may experience mild ketosis on a low-carb diet.

3.Calorie Intake
Low-carb diets and the keto diet both involve reducing carbohydrate intake, but they may differ in terms of overall calorie intake. Low-carb diets often involve reducing calorie intake to create a calorie deficit, which can lead to weight loss. In contrast, the keto diet may not require a calorie deficit, as the high fat intake can help individuals feel full and satisfied, leading to a natural reduction in calorie intake.

4.Health Benefits

Both low-carb diets and the keto diet have been associated with various health benefits, including weight loss, improved blood sugar control, and reduced inflammation. However, the keto diet may offer additional benefits, such as improved mental clarity and cognitive function due to the increased production of ketones in the brain.

5.Food Choices

Both low-carb diets and the keto diet involve restricting carbohydrate intake, but the types of foods that are allowed may differ. Low-carb diets often allow for a wider variety of foods, including some fruits, starchy vegetables, and whole grains. In contrast, the keto diet requires very strict carbohydrate restriction, which may limit food choices and require careful planning to ensure adequate nutrient intake.

In summary, while low-carb diets and the keto diet share some similarities in terms of carbohydrate restriction, they differ in terms of macronutrient ratios, ketosis induction, calorie intake, health benefits, and food choices.

What Are The Benefits of The Keto Diet?

1.Weight Loss

The keto diet can be an effective way to lose weight, as it encourages the body to burn fat for fuel instead of carbohydrates. By reducing carbohydrate intake and increasing fat intake, the body enters a state of ketosis, in which it burns stored fat for energy. This can lead to significant weight loss, particularly in the first few weeks of the diet.

2.Reduced inflammation

Chronic inflammation has been linked to a range of health problems, including heart disease, cancer, and autoimmune disorders. The keto diet has been shown to reduce inflammation in the body, which may help to prevent these conditions.

3.Improved cardiovascular health

The keto diet may also have benefits for cardiovascular health. By reducing carbohydrate intake and increasing fat intake, the diet can improve cholesterol levels, reduce triglycerides, and lower blood pressure.

4.Increased energy levels

Many individuals report increased energy levels on the keto diet, as the body burns fat for fuel instead of carbohydrates. In addition, the diet may improve mental clarity and cognitive function, particularly in individuals with neurological disorders such as epilepsy.

5.Reduced hunger and cravings

The high fat intake on the keto diet can help individuals feel full and satisfied, reducing hunger and cravings. This can make it easier to stick to the diet and avoid overeating.

6.Potential cancer-fighting properties

Some research has suggested that the keto diet may have anti-cancer properties, as it may reduce the growth and spread of cancer cells. However, more research is needed in this area.

Can the Keto Diet Reverse Type 2 Diabetes?

Type 2 diabetes is a chronic condition that affects millions of people worldwide. It is characterized by high blood sugar levels due to insulin resistance, which occurs when the body becomes less responsive to insulin. While there is no cure for type 2 diabetes, it can be managed through lifestyle changes, including diet and exercise. The keto diet is one approach that has been shown to have potential benefits for individuals with type 2 diabetes.

The keto diet is a low-carbohydrate, high-fat diet that is designed to induce a state of ketosis, in which the body burns fat for fuel instead of carbohydrates. By limiting carbohydrate intake to a very low level, the body is forced to produce ketones from fat stores, which can be used as an alternative fuel source.

One of the benefits of the keto diet is its potential to improve blood sugar control. By reducing carbohydrate intake and increasing fat intake, the body produces less insulin, which can help to lower blood sugar levels. In addition, the diet may reduce insulin resistance, which is a key factor in the development of type 2 diabetes.

Several studies have investigated the effects of the keto diet on individuals with type 2 diabetes. A 2017 study published in the journal Nutrition & Diabetes found that a 12-week keto diet resulted in significant improvements in blood sugar control, as well as reductions in medication use in individuals with type 2 diabetes. Another study published in the Journal of Medical Internet Research found that a low-carbohydrate, high-fat diet was more effective at improving blood sugar control than a low-fat diet in individuals with type 2 diabetes.

However, it is important to note that the keto diet may not be suitable for everyone with type 2 diabetes. Individuals who are on insulin or other diabetes medications should consult with their healthcare provider before starting the diet, as it may require adjustments to medication dosages. In addition, the keto diet may not be sustainable in the long term for some individuals, as it can be challenging to maintain a very low carbohydrate intake over time.

Overall, the keto diet has shown promise as a potential tool for managing type 2 diabetes. However, more research is needed to fully understand its effects on blood sugar control, medication use, and long-term sustainability. Individuals with type 2 diabetes should work with their healthcare provider to determine the best approach for managing their condition, which may include dietary changes, medication, and lifestyle modifications.

What to Eat and Avoid on The Keto Diet?

Foods to Eat:

1.Meat: Beef, pork, chicken, turkey, lamb, and other meats are allowed on the keto diet.

2.Fish and seafood: Salmon, tuna, mackerel, shrimp, crab, and other seafood are good sources of protein and healthy fats.

3.Eggs: Eggs are a staple on the keto diet and can be consumed in a variety of ways, including fried, scrambled, boiled, or baked.

4.Low-carbohydrate vegetables: Non-starchy vegetables such as spinach, kale, broccoli, cauliflower, and zucchini are allowed on the keto diet.

5.Nuts and seeds: Almonds, walnuts, pecans, chia seeds, and flaxseeds are all good sources of healthy fats and protein.

6.High-fat dairy: Butter, cream, cheese, and other high-fat dairy products are allowed in moderation on the keto diet.

7.Oils and fats: Olive oil, coconut oil, avocado oil, and other healthy fats are allowed on the keto diet.

Foods to Avoid:

1.Grains and starches: Bread, pasta, rice, cereal, and other starchy foods are not allowed on the keto diet.

2.Sugary foods: Candy, soda, fruit juice, and other sugary foods should be avoided on the keto diet.

3.Fruit: Most fruits are high in carbohydrates and should be avoided on the keto diet, although small amounts of berries can be consumed in moderation.

4.Beans and legumes: Chickpeas, lentils, and other beans and legumes are high in carbohydrates and should be avoided on the keto diet.

5.Sweetened dairy products: Flavored yogurt, sweetened creamers, and other sweetened dairy products should be avoided on the keto diet.

6.High-carbohydrate vegetables: Potatoes, corn, peas, and other high-carbohydrate vegetables should be limited on the keto diet.

7.Processed foods: Processed foods such as chips, crackers, and other snack foods are not allowed on the keto diet.

How to Get Started with A Keto Diet?

1.Choose a cookbook

There are many keto diet cookbooks available, so it is important to choose one that suits your needs and preferences. Look for a cookbook that includes a variety of recipes and meal ideas, as well as tips for following the keto diet.

2.Follow the recipes

When preparing your meals, follow the recipes in the cookbook carefully, paying attention to the recommended macronutrient ratios and serving sizes. This will ensure that you are getting enough healthy fats and staying within your recommended carbohydrate intake.

3.Monitor your ketone levels

To ensure that you are in a state of ketosis, it may be helpful to monitor your ketone levels using a blood ketone meter. This can help you track your progress and make adjustments to your diet if necessary.

4.Stay hydrated

Drinking plenty of water is important on the keto diet, as it can help to prevent dehydration and support overall health.

5.Be patient

It can take time for your body to adjust to the keto diet and enter a state of ketosis. It is important to be patient and stick with the diet, even if you experience some initial side effects such as the "keto flu" or cravings for high-carbohydrate foods.

Overall, using a keto diet cookbook can be a helpful way to get started with the keto diet, as it provides you with a variety of recipes and meal ideas to choose from. By following the recipes carefully and monitoring your ketone levels, you can ensure that you are getting the most out of the diet and achieving your health goals.

BASIC KITCHEN CONVERSIONS & EQUIVALENTS

DRY MEASUREMENTS CONVERSION CHART

3 TEASPOONS = 1 TABLESPOON = 1/16 CUP

6 TEASPOONS = 2 TABLESPOONS = 1/8 CUP

12 TEASPOONS = 4 TABLESPOONS = 1/4 CUP

24 TEASPOONS = 8 TABLESPOONS = 1/2 CUP

36 TEASPOONS = 12 TABLESPOONS = 3/4 CUP

48 TEASPOONS = 16 TABLESPOONS = 1 CUP

METRIC TO US COOKING CONVERSIONS

OVEN TEMPERATURES

120 °C = 250 °F

160 °C = 320 °F

180° C = 350 °F

205 °C = 400 °F

220 °C = 425 °F

LIQUID MEASUREMENTS CONVERSION CHART

8 FLUID OUNCES = 1 CUP = 1/2 PINT = 1/4 QUART

16 FLUID OUNCES = 2 CUPS = 1 PINT = 1/2 QUART

32 FLUID OUNCES = 4 CUPS = 2 PINTS = 1 QUART

 = 1/4 GALLON

128 FLUID OUNCES = 16 CUPS = 8 PINTS = 4 QUARTS = 1 GALLON

BAKING IN GRAMS

1 CUP FLOUR = 140 GRAMS

1 CUP SUGAR = 150 GRAMS

1 CUP POWDERED SUGAR = 160 GRAMS

1 CUP HEAVY CREAM = 235 GRAMS

VOLUME

1 MILLILITER = 1/5 TEASPOON

5 ML = 1 TEASPOON

15 ML = 1 TABLESPOON

240 ML = 1 CUP OR 8 FLUID OUNCES

1 LITER = 34 FL. OUNCES

WEIGHT

1 GRAM = .035 OUNCES

100 GRAMS = 3.5 OUNCES

500 GRAMS = 1.1 POUNDS

1 KILOGRAM = 35 OUNCES

US TO METRIC COOKING CONVERSIONS

1/5 TSP = 1 ML

1 TSP = 5 ML

1 TBSP = 15 ML

1 FL OUNCE = 30 ML

1 CUP = 237 ML

1 PINT (2 CUPS) = 473 ML

1 QUART (4 CUPS) = .95 LITER

1 GALLON (16 CUPS) = 3.8 LITERS

1 OZ = 28 GRAMS

1 POUND = 454 GRAMS

BUTTER

1 CUP BUTTER = 2 STICKS = 8 OUNCES = 230 GRAMS = 8 TABLESPOONS

WHAT DOES 1 CUP EQUAL

1 CUP = 8 FLUID OUNCES

1 CUP = 16 TABLESPOONS

1 CUP = 48 TEASPOONS

1 CUP = 1/2 PINT

1 CUP = 1/4 QUART

1 CUP = 1/16 GALLON

1 CUP = 240 ML

BAKING PAN CONVERSIONS

1 CUP ALL-PURPOSE FLOUR = 4.5 OZ

1 CUP ROLLED OATS = 3 OZ 1 LARGE EGG = 1.7 OZ

1 CUP BUTTER = 8 OZ 1 CUP MILK = 8 OZ

1 CUP HEAVY CREAM = 8.4 OZ

1 CUP GRANULATED SUGAR = 7.1 OZ

1 CUP PACKED BROWN SUGAR = 7.75 OZ

1 CUP VEGETABLE OIL = 7.7 OZ

1 CUP UNSIFTED POWDERED SUGAR = 4.4 OZ

BAKING PAN CONVERSIONS

9-INCH ROUND CAKE PAN = 12 CUPS

10-INCH TUBE PAN = 16 CUPS

11-INCH BUNDT PAN = 12 CUPS

9-INCH SPRINGFORM PAN = 10 CUPS

9 X 5 INCH LOAF PAN = 8 CUPS

9-INCH SQUARE PAN = 8 CUPS

Appetizers, Snacks & Side Dishes

Lemony Fried Artichokes

Servings: 4 | Cooking Time: 20 Minutes

Ingredients:

- 12 fresh baby artichokes
- 2 tbsp lemon juice
- 2 tbsp olive oil
- Salt to taste

Directions:

1. Slice the artichokes vertically into narrow wedges. Drain on paper towels before frying.
2. Heat olive oil in a cast-iron skillet over high heat. Fry the artichokes until browned and crispy. Drain excess oil on paper towels. Sprinkle with salt and lemon juice.

Nutrition Info:

- Per Servings 2.9g Carbs, 2g Protein, 2.4g Fat, 35 Calories

Parmesan Crackers

Servings: 6 | Cooking Time: 25 Minutes

Ingredients:

- 1 ⅓ cups coconut flour
- 1 ¼ cup grated Parmesan cheese
- Salt and black pepper to taste
- 1 tsp garlic powder
- ⅓ cup butter, softened
- ⅓ tsp sweet paprika
- ⅓ cup heavy cream
- Water as needed

Directions:

1. Preheat the oven to 350ºF.
2. Mix the coconut flour, parmesan cheese, salt, pepper, garlic powder, and paprika in a bowl. Add in the butter and mix well. Top with the heavy cream and mix again until a smooth, thick mixture has formed. Add 1 to 2 tablespoon of water at this point, if it is too thick.
3. Place the dough on a cutting board and cover with plastic wrap. Use a rolling pin to spread out the dough into a light rectangle. Cut cracker squares out of the dough and arrange them on a baking sheet without overlapping. Bake for 20 minutes and transfer to a serving bowl after.

Nutrition Info:

- Per Servings 0.7g Carbs, 5g Protein, 3g Fat, 115 Calories

Spicy Chicken Cucumber Bites

Servings: 6 | Cooking Time: 5 Minutes

Ingredients:

- 2 cucumbers, sliced with a 3-inch thickness
- 2 cups small dices leftover chicken
- ¼ jalapeño pepper, seeded and minced
- 1 tbsp Dijon mustard
- ⅓ cup mayonnaise
- Salt and black pepper to taste

Directions:

1. Cut mid-level holes in cucumber slices with a knife and set aside. Combine chicken, jalapeno pepper, mustard, mayonnaise, salt, and black pepper to be evenly mixed. Fill cucumber holes with chicken mixture and serve.

Nutrition Info:

- Per Servings 0g Carbs, 10g Protein, 14g Fat, 170 Calories

Cobb Salad With Blue Cheese Dressing

Servings: 6 | Cooking Time: 2 Hours 40 Minutes

Ingredients:

- ½ cup buttermilk
- 1 cup mayonnaise
- 2 tbsp sugar-free Worcestershire sauce
- ½ cup sour cream
- 1 ½ cup crumbled blue cheese
- Salt and black pepper to taste
- 2 tbsp chopped chives
- 6 eggs
- 1 cup water
- Ice bath
- 2 chicken breasts, boneless and skinless
- Salt and black pepper to taste
- 5 strips bacon
- 1 iceberg lettuce, cut into chunks
- 1 romaine lettuce, chopped
- 1 bibb lettuce, cored and leaves removed
- 2 avocado, pitted and diced
- 2 large tomatoes, chopped
- ½ cup crumbled blue cheese
- 2 scallions, chopped

Directions:

1. In a bowl, whisk the buttermilk, mayonnaise, Worcestershire sauce, and sour cream. Stir in the blue cheese, salt, pepper, and chives. Place in the refrigerator to chill for 2 hours.
2. Bring the eggs to boil in salted water over medium heat for 10 minutes. Once ready, drain the eggs and transfer to the ice bath. Peel and chop the eggs. Set aside.
3. Preheat the grill pan over high heat. Season the chicken with salt and pepper. Grill for 3 minutes on each side. Remove to a plate to cool for 3 minutes, and cut into bite-size chunks.
4. Fry the bacon in another pan set over medium heat until crispy, about 6 minutes. Remove, let cool for 2 minutes, and chop.
5. Arrange the lettuce leaves in a salad bowl and in single piles, add the avocado, tomatoes, eggs, bacon, and chicken. Sprinkle the blue cheese over the salad as well as the scallions and black pepper.
6. Drizzle the blue cheese dressing on the salad and serve with low carb bread.

Nutrition Info:

- Per Servings 2g Carbs, 23g Protein, 14g Fat, 122 Calories

Bacon Jalapeno Poppers

Servings: 8 | Cooking Time: 10 Minutes

Ingredients:

- 4-ounce cream cheese
- ¼ cup cheddar cheese, shredded
- 1 teaspoon paprika
- 16 fresh jalapenos, sliced lengthwise and seeded
- 16 strips of uncured bacon, cut into half
- Salt and pepper to taste

Directions:

1. Preheat oven to 400oF.
2. In a mixing bowl, mix the cream cheese, cheddar cheese, salt, and paprika until well-combined.
3. Scoop half a teaspoon onto each half of jalapeno peppers.
4. Use a thin strip of bacon and wrap it around the cheese-filled jalapeno half.
5. Place in a single layer in a lightly greased baking sheet and roast for 10 minutes.
6. Serve and enjoy.

Nutrition Info:

- Per Servings 3.2g Carbs, 10.6g Protein, 18.9g Fat, 225 Calories

Ricotta And Pomegranate

Servings: 3 | Cooking Time: 12 Minutes

Ingredients:

- 1 cup Ricotta cheese
- 3 tablespoons olive oil
- 1/2 cup pomegranate Arils
- 2 tsp thyme, fresh
- 2 cups arugula leaves
- Pepper and salt to taste
- 1/2 tsp grated lemon zest

Directions:

1. Mix all ingredients in a bowl.
2. Toss until well combined.
3. Season with pepper and salt.
4. Serve and enjoy.

Nutrition Info:

- Per Servings 9g Carbs, 11g Protein, 25g Fat, 312 Calories

Choco And Coconut Bars

Servings: 9 | Cooking Time: 30 Minutes

Ingredients:

- 1 tbsp Stevia
- ¾ cup shredded coconut, unsweetened
- ½ cup ground nuts (almonds, pecans, or walnuts)
- ¼ cup unsweetened cocoa powder
- 4 tbsp coconut oil

Directions:

1. In a medium bowl, mix shredded coconut, nuts, and cocoa powder.
2. Add Stevia and coconut oil.
3. Mix batter thoroughly.
4. In a 9x9 square inch pan or dish, press the batter and for a 30-minutes place in the freezer.
5. Evenly divide into suggested servings and enjoy.

Nutrition Info:

- Per Servings 2.7g Carbs, 1.3g Protein, 9.3g Fat, 99.7 Calories

Balsamic Zucchini

Servings: 4 | Cooking Time: 20 Minutes

Ingredients:

- 3 medium zucchinis, cut into thin slices
- 1/2 cup chopped sweet onion
- 1/2 teaspoon dried rosemary, crushed
- 2 tablespoons balsamic vinegar
- 1/3 cup crumbled feta cheese
- 1/2 teaspoon salt
- 1/4 teaspoon pepper
- 4 tablespoon olive oil

Directions:

1. In a large skillet, heat oil over medium-high heat; sauté zucchini and onion until crisp-tender, 6-8 minutes. Stir in seasonings. Add vinegar; cook and stir 2 minutes. Top with cheese.

Nutrition Info:

- Per Servings 5g Carbs, 4g Protein, 16g Fat, 175 Calories

Crispy Keto Pork Bites

Servings: 3 | Cooking Time: 30 Minutes

Ingredients:

- ½ pork belly, sliced to thin strips
- 1 tablespoon butter
- 1 onion, diced
- 4 tablespoons coconut cream
- Salt and pepper to taste

Directions:

1. Place all ingredients in a mixing bowl and allow to marinate in the fridge for 2 hours.
2. When 2 hours is nearly up, preheat oven to 400oF and lightly grease a cookie sheet with cooking spray.
3. Place the pork strips in an even layer on the cookie sheet.
4. Roast for 30 minutes and turnover halfway through cooking.

Nutrition Info:

- Per Servings 1.9g Carbs, 19.1g Protein, 40.6g Fat, 448 Calories

Sweet And Hot Nuts

Servings: 12 | Cooking Time: 4 Hours

Ingredients:

- ½ pound assorted nuts, raw
- 1/3 cup butter, melted
- 1 teaspoon cayenne pepper or to taste
- 1 tablespoon MCT oil or coconut oil
- 1 packet stevia powder
- ¼ tsp salt

Directions:

1. Place all ingredients in the crockpot.
2. Give it a good stir to combine everything.
3. Close the lid and cook on low for 4 hours.

Nutrition Info:

- Per Servings 2.9g Carbs, 7.0g Protein, 21.6g Fat, 271 Calories

Easy Garlic Keto Bread

Servings: 1 | Cooking Time: 1 Minute 30 Seconds

Ingredients:

- 1 large egg
- 1 tbsp milk
- 1 tbsp coconut flour
- 1 tbsp almond flour
- ¼ tsp baking powder
- Salt to taste

Directions:

1. Mix all ingredients in a bowl until well combined.
2. Pour into a mug and place in the microwave oven.
3. Cook for 1 minute and 30 seconds.
4. Once cooked, invert the mug.
5. Allow to cool before slicing.

Nutrition Info:

- Per Servings 3g Carbs, 4g Protein, 7g Fat, 75 Calories

Devilled Eggs With Sriracha Mayo

Servings: 4 | Cooking Time: 15 Minutes

Ingredients:

- 8 large eggs
- 3 cups water
- Ice water bath
- 3 tbsp sriracha sauce
- 4 tbsp mayonnaise
- Salt to taste
- ¼ tsp smoked paprika

Directions:

1. Bring eggs to boil in salted water in a pot over high heat, and then reduce the heat to simmer for 10 minutes. Transfer eggs to an ice water bath, let cool completely and peel the shells.
2. Slice the eggs in half height wise and empty the yolks into a bowl. Smash with a fork and mix in sriracha sauce, mayonnaise, and half of the paprika until smooth.
3. Spoon filling into a piping bag with a round nozzle and fill the egg whites to be slightly above the brim. Garnish with remaining paprika and serve immediately.

Nutrition Info:

- Per Servings 1g Carbs, 4g Protein, 19g Fat, 195 Calories

Air Fryer Garlic Chicken Wings

Servings: 4 | Cooking Time: 25 Minutes

Ingredients:

- 16 pieces chicken wings
- ¾ cup almond flour
- 4 tablespoons minced garlic
- ¼ cup butter, melted
- 2 tablespoons Stevia powder
- Salt and pepper to taste

Directions:

1. Preheat oven to 400oF.
2. In a mixing bowl, combine the chicken wings, almond flour, Stevia powder, and garlic. Season with salt and pepper to taste.
3. Place in a lightly greased cookie sheet in an even layer and cook for 25 minutes.
4. Halfway through the cooking time, turnover chicken.
5. Once cooked, place in a bowl and drizzle with melted butter. Toss to coat.
6. Serve and enjoy.

Nutrition Info:

- Per Servings 7.8g Carbs, 23.7g Protein, 26.9g Fat, 365 Calories

Cheesy Chicken Fritters With Dill Dip

Servings: 4 | Cooking Time: 40 Minutes + Cooling Time

Ingredients:

- 1 lb chicken breasts, thinly sliced
- 1 ¼ cup mayonnaise
- ¼ cup coconut flour
- 2 eggs
- Salt and black pepper to taste
- 1 cup grated mozzarella cheese
- 4 tbsp chopped dill
- 3 tbsp olive oil
- 1 cup sour cream
- 1 tsp garlic powder
- 1 tbsp chopped parsley
- 2 tbsp finely chopped onion

Directions:

1. In a bowl, mix 1 cup of the mayonnaise, 3 tbsp of dill, sour cream, garlic powder, onion, and salt. Cover the bowl with plastic wrap and refrigerate for 30 minutes.
2. Mix the chicken, remaining mayonnaise, coconut flour, eggs, salt, pepper, mozzarella, and remaining dill, in a bowl. Cover the bowl with plastic wrap and refrigerate it for 2 hours. After the marinating time is over, remove from the fridge.
3. Place a skillet over medium fire and heat the olive oil. Fetch 2 tablespoons of chicken mixture into the skillet, use the back of a spatula to flatten the top. Cook for 4 minutes, flip, and fry for 4 more.
4. Remove onto a wire rack and repeat the cooking process until the batter is finished, adding more oil as needed. Garnish the fritters with parsley and serve with dill dip.

Nutrition Info:

- Per Servings 0.8g Carbs, 12g Protein, 7g Fat, 151 Calories

Apricot And Soy Nut Trail Mix

Servings: 20 | Cooking Time: 10 Minutes

Ingredients:

- ¼ cup dried apricots, chopped
- 1 cup pumpkin seeds
- ½ cup roasted cashew nuts
- 1 cup roasted, shelled pistachios
- Salt to taste
- 3 tbsp MCT oil or coconut oil

Directions:

1. In a medium mixing bowl, place all ingredients.
2. Thoroughly combine.
3. Bake in the oven for 10 minutes at 3750F.
4. In 20 small zip-top bags, get ¼ cup of the mixture and place in each bag.
5. One zip-top bag is equal to one serving.
6. If properly stored, this can last up to two weeks.

Nutrition Info:

- Per Servings 4.6g Carbs, 5.2g Protein, 10.75g Fat, 129 Calories

Cheesy Green Bean Crisps

Servings: 6 | Cooking Time: 30 Minutes

Ingredients:

- Cooking spray
- ¼ cup shredded pecorino romano cheese
- ¼ cup pork rind crumbs
- 1 tsp garlic powder
- Salt and black pepper to taste
- 2 eggs
- 1 lb green beans, thread removed

Directions:

1. Preheat oven to 425°F and line two baking sheets with foil. Grease with cooking spray and set aside.
2. Mix the pecorino, pork rinds, garlic powder, salt, and black pepper in a bowl. Beat the eggs in another bowl. Coat green beans in eggs, then cheese mixture and arrange evenly on the baking sheets.
3. Grease lightly with cooking spray and bake for 15 minutes to be crispy. Transfer to a wire rack to cool before serving. Serve with sugar-free tomato dip.

Nutrition Info:

- Per Servings 3g Carbs, 5g Protein, 19g Fat, 210 Calories

Crispy Chorizo With Cheesy Topping

Servings: 6 | Cooking Time: 30 Minutes

Ingredients:

- 7 ounces Spanish chorizo
- 4 ounces cream cheese
- ¼ cup chopped parsley

Directions:

1. Preheat your oven to 325 °F. Slice the chorizo into 30 slices
2. Line a baking dish with waxed paper. Bake the chorizo for 15 minutes until crispy. Remove from the oven and let cool. Arrange on a serving platter. Top each slice with some cream cheese.
3. Serve sprinkled with chopped parsley.

Nutrition Info:

- Per Servings 0g Carbs, 5g Protein, 13g Fat, 172 Calories

Tofu Stuffed Peppers

Servings: 8 | Cooking Time: 10 Minutes

Ingredients:

- 1 package firm tofu, crumbled
- 1 onion, finely chopped
- ½ teaspoon turmeric powder
- 1 teaspoon coriander powder
- 8 banana peppers, top-end sliced and seeded
- Salt and pepper to taste
- 3 tablespoons oil

Directions:

1. Preheat oven to 400oF.
2. In a mixing bowl, combine the tofu, onion, coconut oil, turmeric powder, red chili powder, coriander powder, and salt. Mix until well-combined.
3. Scoop the tofu mixture into the hollows of the banana peppers.
4. Place the stuffed peppers in one layer in a lightly greased baking sheet.
5. Cook for 10 minutes.
6. Serve and enjoy.

Nutrition Info:

- Per Servings 4.1g Carbs, 1.2g Protein, 15.6g Fat, 187 Calories

Keto-approved Trail Mix

Servings: 8 | Cooking Time: 3 Minutes

Ingredients:

- ¼ cup salted pumpkin seeds
- ½ cup slivered almonds
- ¾ cup roasted pecan halves
- ¼ cup unsweetened cranberries
- ¾ cup toasted coconut flakes

Directions:

1. In a skillet, place almonds and pecans. Heat for 2-3 minutes and let it cool.
2. Once cooled, in a large resealable plastic bag, combine all ingredients.
3. Seal and shake vigorously to mix.
4. Serve and enjoy.

Nutrition Info:

- Per Servings 8.0g Carbs, 4.4g Protein, 14.4g Fat, 184 Calories

Cajun Spiced Pecans

Servings: 10 | Cooking Time: 10 Minutes

Ingredients:

- 1-pound pecan halves
- ¼ cup butter
- 1 packet Cajun seasoning mix
- ¼ teaspoon ground cayenne pepper
- Salt and pepper to taste

Directions:

1. Place a nonstick saucepan on medium fire and melt butter.
2. Add pecans and remaining ingredients.
3. Sauté for 5 minutes.
4. Remove from fire and let it cool completely.
5. Serve and enjoy.

Nutrition Info:

- Per Servings 6.8g Carbs, 4.2g Protein, 37.3g Fat, 356.5 Calories

Easy Baked Parmesan Chips

Servings: 10 | Cooking Time: 10 Minutes

Ingredients:

- 1 cup grated Parmesan cheese, low fat
- 1 tablespoon olive oil

Directions:

1. Lightly grease a cookie sheet and preheat oven to 400°F.
2. Evenly sprinkle parmesan cheese on a cookie sheet into 10 circles. Place them about ½-inch apart.
3. Drizzle with oil
4. Bake until lightly browned and crisped.
5. Let it cool, evenly divide into suggested servings and enjoy.

Nutrition Info:

- Per Servings 1.4g Carbs, 2.8g Protein, 12.8g Fat, 142 Calories

Balsamic Brussels Sprouts With Prosciutto

Servings: 4 | Cooking Time: 40 Minutes

Ingredients:

- 3 tbsp balsamic vinegar
- 1 tbsp erythritol
- ½ tbsp olive oil
- Salt and black pepper to taste
- 1 lb Brussels sprouts, halved
- 5 slices prosciutto, chopped

Directions:

1. Preheat oven to 400°F and line a baking sheet with parchment paper. Mix balsamic vinegar, erythritol, olive oil, salt, and black pepper and combine with the brussels sprouts in a bowl.
2. Spread the mixture on the baking sheet and roast for 30 minutes until tender on the inside and crispy on the outside. Toss with prosciutto, share among 4 plates, and serve with chicken breasts.

Nutrition Info:

- Per Servings 0g Carbs, 8g Protein, 14g Fat, 166 Calories

Cocoa Nuts Goji Bars

Servings: 6 | Cooking Time: 5 Minutes

Ingredients:

- 1 cup raw almonds
- 1 cup raw walnuts
- ¼ tsp cinnamon powder
- ¼ cup dried goji berries
- 1 ½ tsp vanilla extract
- 2 tbsp unsweetened chocolate chips
- 2 tbsp coconut oil
- 1 tbsp golden flax meal
- 1 tsp erythritol

Directions:

1. Combine the walnuts and almonds in the food processor and process at high-speed to be smooth. Add the cinnamon powder, goji berries, vanilla extract, chocolate chips, coconut oil, golden flax meal, and erythritol. Process further until the mixture begins to stick to each other, about 2 minutes.
2. Spread out a large piece of plastic wrap on a flat surface and place the dough on it. Wrap the dough and use a rolling pin to spread it out into a thick rectangle.
3. Unwrap the dough after and use an oiled knife to cut the dough into bars.

Nutrition Info:

- Per Servings 6g Carbs, 2g Protein, 11g Fat, 170 Calories

Coconut Ginger Macaroons

Servings: 6 | Cooking Time: 20 Minutes

Ingredients:

- 2 fingers ginger root, peeled and pureed
- 6 egg whites
- 1 cup finely shredded coconut
- ¼ cup swerve
- A pinch of chili powder
- 1 cup water
- Angel hair chili to garnish

Directions:

1. Preheat the oven to 350ºF and line a baking sheet with parchment paper. Set aside.
2. Then, in a heatproof bowl, whisk the ginger, egg whites, shredded coconut, swerve, and chili powder.
3. Bring the water to boil in a pot over medium heat and place the heatproof bowl on the pot. Then, continue whisking the mixture until it is glossy, about 4 minutes. Do not let the bowl touch the water or be too hot so that the eggs don't cook.
4. Spoon the mixture into the piping bag after and pipe out 40 to 50 little mounds on the lined baking sheet. Bake the macaroons in the middle part of the oven for 15 minutes.
5. Once they are ready, transfer them to a wire rack, garnish them with the angel hair chili, and serve.

Nutrition Info:

- Per Servings 0.3g Carbs, 6.8g Protein, 3.5g Fat, 97 Calories

Pecorino-mushroom Balls

Servings: 4 | Cooking Time: 20 Minutes

Ingredients:

- 2 tbsp butter, softened
- 2 garlic cloves, minced
- 2 cups portobello mushrooms, chopped
- 4 tbsp blanched almond flour
- 4 tbsp ground flax seeds
- 4 tbsp hemp seeds
- 4 tbsp sunflower seeds
- 1 tbsp cajun seasonings
- 1 tsp mustard
- 2 eggs, whisked
- ½ cup pecorino cheese

Directions:

1. Set a pan over medium-high heat and warm 1 tablespoon of butter. Add in mushrooms and garlic and sauté until there is no more water in mushrooms.
2. Place in pecorino cheese, almond flour, hemp seeds, mustard, eggs, sunflower seeds, flax seeds, and Cajun seasonings. Create 4 burgers from the mixture.
3. In a pan, warm the remaining butter; fry the burgers for 7 minutes. Flip them over with a wide spatula and cook for 6 more minutes. Serve while warm.

Nutrition Info:

- Per Servings 7.7g Carbs, 16.8g Protein, 30g Fat, 370 Calories

Poultry Recipes

Poultry Recipes

Pacific Chicken

Servings: 6 | Cooking Time: 50 Minutes

Ingredients:

- 4 chicken breasts
- Salt and black pepper, to taste
- ½ cup mayonnaise
- 3 tbsp Dijon mustard
- 1 tsp xylitol
- ¾ cup pork rinds
- ¾ cup grated Grana-Padano cheese
- 2 tsp garlic powder
- 1 tsp onion powder
- ¼ tsp salt
- ¼ tsp black pepper
- 8 pieces ham, sliced
- 4 slices gruyere cheese

Directions:

1. Set an oven to 350ºF and grease a baking dish. Using a small bowl, place in the pork rinds and crush. Add chicken to a plate and season well.
2. In a separate bowl, mix mustard, mayonnaise, and xylitol. Take about ¼ of this mixture and spread over the chicken. Preserve the rest. Take ½ pork rinds, seasonings, most of Grana-Padano cheese, and place to the bottom of the baking dish. Add the chicken to the top.
3. Cover the chicken with the remaining Grana-Padano, pork rinds, and seasonings. Place in the oven for about 40 minutes until the chicken is cooked completely. Take out from the oven and top with gruyere cheese and ham. Place back in the oven and cook until golden brown.

Nutrition Info:

- Per Servings 2.6g Carbs, 33g Protein, 31g Fat, 465 Calories

Pesto Chicken

Servings: 4 | Cooking Time: 30 Minutes

Ingredients:

- 2 cups basil leaves
- ¼ cup + 1 tbsp extra virgin olive oil, divided
- 5 sun-dried tomatoes
- 4 chicken breasts
- 6 cloves garlic, smashed, peeled, and minced
- What you'll need from the store cupboard:
- Salt and pepper to taste
- Water

Directions:

1. Put in the food processor the basil leaves, ¼ cup olive oil, and tomatoes. Season with salt and pepper to taste. Add a cup of water if needed.
2. Season chicken breasts with pepper and salt generously.
3. On medium fire, heat a saucepan for 2 minutes. Add a tbsp of olive oil to the pan and swirl to coat bottom and sides. Heat oil for a minute.
4. Add chicken and sear for 5 minutes per side.
5. Add pesto sauce, cover, and cook on low fire for 15 minutes or until chicken is cooked thoroughly.
6. Serve and enjoy.

Nutrition Info:

- Per Servings 1.1g Carbs, 60.8g Protein, 32.7g Fat, 556 Calories

Turkey Enchilada Bowl

Servings: 4 | Cooking Time: 30 Minutes

Ingredients:

- 2 tbsp coconut oil
- 1 lb boneless, skinless turkey thighs, cut into pieces
- ¾ cup red enchilada sauce (sugar-free)
- ¼ cup water
- ¼ cup chopped onion
- 3 oz canned diced green chilis
- 1 avocado, diced
- 1 cup shredded mozzarella cheese
- ¼ cup chopped pickled jalapeños
- ½ cup sour cream
- 1 tomato, diced

Directions:

1. Set a large pan over medium-high heat. Add coconut oil and warm. Place in the turkey and cook until browned on the outside. Stir in onion, chillis, water, and enchilada sauce, then close with a lid.
2. Allow simmering for 20 minutes until the turkey is cooked through. Spoon the turkey on a serving bowl and top with the sauce, cheese, sour cream, tomato, and avocado.

Nutrition Info:

- Per Servings 5.9g Carbs, 38g Protein, 40.2g Fat, 568 Calories

Chicken And Mushrooms

Servings: 6 | Cooking Time: 30 Minutes

Ingredients:

- 6 boneless chicken breasts, halved
- 1 onion, chopped
- 4 cloves of garlic, minced
- ½ cup coconut milk
- 1 cup mushrooms, sliced
- Pepper and salt to taste
- ½ cup water

Directions:

1. On high fire, heat a saucepan for 2 minutes. Add oil to the pan and swirl to coat bottom and sides. Heat oil for a minute.
2. Add chicken and sear for 4 minutes per side. Transfer chicken to a chopping board and chop into bite-sized chunks.
3. In the same pan, lower fire to medium and sauté garlic for a minute. Add onion and sauté for 3 minutes. Stir in mushrooms and water. Deglaze pot.
4. Return chicken to the pot and mix well. Season with pepper and salt.
5. Cover and lower fire to simmer and cook for 15 minutes.

Nutrition Info:

- Per Servings 3.5g Carbs, 62.2g Protein, 11.9g Fat, 383 Calories

Chicken, Eggplant And Gruyere Gratin

Servings: 4 | Cooking Time: 55 Minutes

Ingredients:

- 3 tbsp butter
- 1 eggplant, chopped
- 2 tbsp gruyere cheese, grated
- Salt and black pepper, to taste
- 2 garlic cloves, minced
- 6 chicken thighs

Directions:

1. Set a pan over medium heat and warm 1 tablespoon butter, place in the chicken thighs, season with pepper and salt, cook each side for 3 minutes and lay them in a baking dish. In the same pan melt the rest of the butter and cook the garlic for 1 minute.
2. Stir in the eggplant, pepper, and salt, and cook for 10 minutes. Ladle this mixture over the chicken, spread with the cheese, set in the oven at 350°F, and bake for 30 minutes. Turn on the oven's broiler, and broil everything for 2 minutes. Split among serving plates and enjoy.

Nutrition Info:

- Per Servings 5g Carbs, 34g Protein, 37g Fat, 412 Calories

Rotisserie Chicken With Garlic Paprika

Servings: 12 | Cooking Time: 1 Hour And 40 Minutes

Ingredients:

- 1 whole chicken
- 1 tbsp. thyme
- 1 tbsp. paprika
- 6 cloves garlic
- 2 bay leaves
- 1 tsp salt
- ½ tbsp pepper

Directions:

1. In a small bowl, mix well thyme, paprika, salt, and pepper.
2. Rub and massage the entire chicken and inside the cavity with the spices.
3. Smash and peel 6 garlic cloves and mince. Rub all over chicken and inside of the chicken.
4. Smash remaining garlic and place in the chicken cavity along with bay leaves.
5. Place chicken on a wire rack placed on top of a baking pan. Tent with foil.
6. Pop in a preheated 350oF oven and bake for 60 minutes.
7. Remove foil and continue baking for another 30 minutes.
8. Let chicken rest for 10 minutes before serving and enjoy.

Nutrition Info:

- Per Servings 1.4g Carbs, 21.3g Protein, 17.2g Fat, 249 Calories

Basil Turkey Meatballs

Servings: 4 | Cooking Time: 15 Minutes

Ingredients:

- 1 pound ground turkey
- 2 tbsp chopped sun-dried tomatoes
- 2 tbsp chopped basil
- ½ tsp garlic powder
- 1 egg
- ½ tsp salt
- ¼ cup almond flour
- 2 tbsp olive oil
- ½ cup shredded mozzarella
- ¼ tsp pepper

Directions:

1. Place everything except the oil in a bowl. Mix with your hands until combined. Form 16 meatballs out of the mixture. Heat the olive oil in a skillet over medium heat. Cook the meatballs for 3 minutes per each side.

Nutrition Info:

- Per Servings 2g Carbs, 22g Protein, 26g Fat, 310 Calories

Quattro Formaggi Chicken

Servings: 8 | Cooking Time: 40 Minutes

Ingredients:

- 3 pounds chicken breasts
- 2 ounces mozzarella cheese, cubed
- 2 ounces mascarpone cheese
- 4 ounces cheddar cheese, cubed
- 2 ounces provolone cheese, cubed
- 1 zucchini, shredded
- Salt and ground black pepper, to taste
- 1 tsp garlic, minced
- ½ cup pancetta, cooked and crumbled

Directions:

1. Sprinkle pepper and salt to the zucchini, squeeze well, and place to a bowl. Stir in the pancetta, mascarpone, cheddar cheese, provolone cheese, mozzarella, pepper, and garlic.
2. Cut slits into chicken breasts, apply pepper and salt, and stuff with the zucchini and cheese mixture. Set on a lined baking sheet, place in the oven at 400ºF, and bake for 45 minutes.

Nutrition Info:

- Per Servings 2g Carbs, 51g Protein, 37g Fat, 565 Calories

Baked Pecorino Toscano Chicken

Servings: 4 | Cooking Time: 60 Minutes

Ingredients:

- 4 chicken breasts, skinless and boneless
- ½ cup mayonnaise
- ½ cup buttermilk
- Salt and ground black pepper, to taste
- ¾ cup Pecorino Toscano cheese, grated
- Cooking spray
- 8 mozzarella cheese slices
- 1 tsp garlic powder

Directions:

1. Spray a baking dish, add in the chicken breasts, and top 2 mozzarella cheese slices to each piece. Using a bowl, combine the Pecorino cheese, pepper, buttermilk, mayonnaise, salt, and garlic. Sprinkle this over the chicken, set the dish in the oven at 370ºF, and bake for 1 hour.

Nutrition Info:

- Per Servings 6g Carbs, 20g Protein, 24g Fat, 346 Calories

Spinach & Ricotta Stuffed Chicken Breasts

Servings: 3 | Cooking Time: 25 Minutes

Ingredients:

- 1 cup spinach, cooked and chopped
- 3 chicken breasts
- Salt and ground black pepper, to taste
- 4 ounces cream cheese, softened
- 1/2 cup ricotta cheese, crumbled
- 1 garlic clove, peeled and minced
- 1 tbsp coconut oil
- ½ cup white wine

Directions:

1. Using a bowl, combine the ricotta cheese with cream cheese, salt, garlic, pepper, and spinach. Add the chicken breasts on a working surface, cut a pocket in each, stuff them with the spinach mixture, and add more pepper and salt.
2. Set a pan over medium-high heat and warm oil, add the stuffed chicken, cook each side for 5 minutes. Put in a baking tray, drizzle with white wine and 2 tablespoons of water and then place in the oven at 420ºF. Bake for 10 minutes, arrange on a serving plate and serve.

Nutrition Info:

- Per Servings 4g Carbs, 23g Protein, 12g Fat, 305 Calories

Red Wine Chicken

Servings: 4 | Cooking Time: 30 Minutes

Ingredients:

- 3 tbsp coconut oil
- 2 lb chicken breast halves, skinless and boneless
- 3 garlic cloves, minced
- Salt and black pepper, to taste
- 1 cup chicken stock
- 3 tbsp stevia
- ½ cup red wine
- 2 tomatoes, sliced
- 6 mozzarella slices
- Fresh basil, chopped, for serving

Directions:

1. Set a pan over medium-high heat and warm oil, add the chicken, season with pepper and salt, cook until brown. Stir in the stevia, garlic, stock, and red wine, and cook for 10 minutes.
2. Remove to a lined baking sheet and arrange mozzarella cheese slices on top. Broil in the oven over medium heat until cheese melts and lay tomato slices over chicken pieces.
3. Sprinkle with chopped basil to serve.

Nutrition Info:

- Per Servings 4g Carbs, 27g Protein, 12g Fat, 314 Calories

One-pot Chicken With Mushrooms And Spinach

Servings: 4 | Cooking Time: 40 Minutes

Ingredients:

- 4 chicken thighs
- 2 cups mushrooms, sliced
- 1 cup spinach, chopped
- ¼ cup butter
- Salt and black pepper, to taste
- ½ tsp onion powder
- ½ tsp garlic powder
- ½ cup water
- 1 tsp Dijon mustard
- 1 tbsp fresh tarragon, chopped

Directions:

1. Set a pan over medium-high heat and warm half of the butter, place in the thighs, and sprinkle with onion powder, pepper, garlic powder, and salt. Cook each side for 3 minutes and set on a plate.
2. Place the remaining butter to the same pan and warm. Stir in mushrooms and cook for 5 minutes. Place in water and mustard, take the chicken pieces back to the pan, and cook for 15 minutes while covered. Stir in the tarragon and spinach, and cook for 5 minutes.

Nutrition Info:

- Per Servings 1g Carbs, 32g Protein, 23g Fat, 453 Calories

Sweet Garlic Chicken Skewers

Servings: 4 | Cooking Time: 17 Minutes + Time Refrigeration

Ingredients:

- For the Skewers
- 3 tbsp soy sauce
- 1 tbsp ginger-garlic paste
- 2 tbsp swerve brown sugar
- Chili pepper to taste
- 2 tbsp olive oil
- 3 chicken breasts, cut into cubes
- For the Dressing
- ½ cup tahini
- ½ tsp garlic powder
- Pink salt to taste
- ¼ cup warm water

Directions:

1. In a small bowl, whisk the soy sauce, ginger-garlic paste, brown sugar, chili pepper, and olive oil.
2. Put the chicken in a zipper bag, pour the marinade over, seal and shake for an even coat. Marinate in the fridge for 2 hours.
3. Preheat a grill to 400°F and thread the chicken on skewers. Cook for 10 minutes in total with three to four turnings to be golden brown. Plate them. Mix the tahini, garlic powder, salt, and warm water in a bowl. Pour into serving jars.
4. Serve the chicken skewers and tahini dressing with cauli fried rice.

Nutrition Info:

- Per Servings 2g Carbs, 15g Protein, 17.4g Fat, 225 Calories

Paprika Chicken With Cream Sauce

Servings: 4 | Cooking Time: 50 Minutes

Ingredients:

- 1 pound chicken thighs
- Salt and black pepper, to taste
- 1 tsp onion powder
- ¼ cup heavy cream
- 2 tbsp butter
- 2 tbsp sweet paprika

Directions:

1. Using a bowl, combine the paprika with onion powder, pepper, and salt. Season chicken pieces with this mixture and lay on a lined baking sheet; bake for 40 minutes in the oven at 400ºF. Split the chicken in serving plates, and set aside.
2. Add the cooking juices to a skillet over medium heat, and mix with the heavy cream and butter. Cook for 5-6 minutes until the sauce is thickened. Sprinkle the sauce over the chicken and serve.

Nutrition Info:

- Per Servings 2.6g Carbs, 31.3g Protein, 33g Fat, 381 Calories

Chicken Breasts With Walnut Crust

Servings: 4 | Cooking Time: 30 Minutes

Ingredients:

- 1 egg, whisked
- Salt and black pepper, to taste
- 3 tbsp coconut oil
- 1½ cups walnuts, ground
- 4 chicken breast halves, boneless and skinless

Directions:

1. Using a bowl, add in walnuts and the whisked egg in another. Season the chicken, dip in the egg and then in pecans. Warm oil in a pan over medium-high heat and brown the chicken.
2. Remove the chicken pieces to a baking sheet, set in the oven, and bake for 10 minutes at 350º F. Serve topped with lemon slices.

Nutrition Info:

- Per Servings 1.5g Carbs, 35g Protein, 18g Fat, 322 Calories

Easy Creamy Chicken

Servings: 8 | Cooking Time: 15 Minutes

Ingredients:

- 5 tablespoons butter
- 2 cans crushed tomatoes
- 4 cooked chicken breasts, shredded
- 1 teaspoon herb seasoning mix of your choice
- ¼ cup parmesan cheese, grated
- Peppcr and salt to taste

Directions:

1. Place a heavy-bottomed pot on medium-high fire and melt butter. Add tomatoes.
2. Sauté for 5 minutes, season with pepper, salt, and seasoning mix.
3. Stir in chicken. Mix well.
4. Cook until heated through, around 5 minutes.
5. Serve with a sprinkle of parmesan cheese.

Nutrition Info:

- Per Servings 2.3g Carbs, 29.5g Protein, 11.3g Fat, 235 Calories

Chicken And Green Cabbage Casserole

Servings: 4 | Cooking Time: 55 Minutes

Ingredients:

- 3 cups cheddar cheese, grated
- 10 ounces green cabbage, shredded
- 3 chicken breasts, skinless, boneless, cooked, cubed
- 1 cup mayonnaise
- 1 tbsp coconut oil, melted
- ⅓ cup chicken stock
- Salt and ground black pepper, to taste
- Juice of 1 lemon

Directions:

1. Apply oil to a baking dish, and set chicken pieces to the bottom. Spread green cabbage, followed by half of the cheese. Using a bowl, combine the mayonnaise with pepper, stock, lemon juice, and salt.
2. Pour this mixture over the chicken, spread the rest of the cheese, cover with aluminum foil, and bake for 30 minutes in the oven at 350°F. Open the aluminum foil, and cook for 20 more minutes.

Nutrition Info:

- Per Servings 6g Carbs, 25g Protein, 15g Fat, 231 Calories

Chili Turkey Patties With Cucumber Salsa

Servings: 4 | Cooking Time: 30 Minutes

Ingredients:

- 2 spring onions, thinly sliced
- 1 pound ground turkey
- 1 egg
- 2 garlic cloves, minced
- 1 tbsp chopped herbs
- 1 small chili pepper, deseeded and diced
- 2 tbsp ghee
- Cucumber Salsa
- 1 tbsp apple cider vinegar
- 1 tbsp chopped dill
- 1 garlic clove, minced
- 2 cucumbers, grated
- 1 cup sour cream
- 1 jalapeño pepper, minced
- 2 tbsp olive oil

Directions:

1. Place all turkey ingredients, except the ghee, in a bowl. Mix to combine. Make patties out of the mixture. Melt the ghee in a skillet over medium heat. Cook the patties for 3 minutes per side.
2. Place all salsa ingredients in a bowl and mix to combine. Serve the patties topped with salsa.

Nutrition Info:

- Per Servings 5g Carbs, 26g Protein, 38g Fat, 475 Calories

Cilantro Chicken Breasts With Mayo-avocado Sauce

Servings: 4 | Cooking Time: 22 Minutes

Ingredients:

- For the Sauce
- 1 avocado, pitted
- ½ cup mayonnaise
- Salt to taste
- For the Chicken
- 3 tbsp ghee
- 4 chicken breasts
- Pink salt and black pepper to taste
- 1 cup chopped cilantro leaves
- ½ cup chicken broth

Directions:

1. Spoon the avocado, mayonnaise, and salt into a small food processor and puree until smooth sauce is derived. Adjust taste with salt as desired.
2. Pour sauce into a jar and refrigerate while you make the chicken.
3. Melt ghee in a large skillet, season chicken with salt and black pepper and fry for 4 minutes on each side to golden brown. Remove chicken to a plate.
4. Pour the broth in the same skillet and add the cilantro. Bring to simmer covered for 3 minutes and add the chicken. Cover and cook on low heat for 5 minutes until liquid has reduced and chicken is fragrant. Dish chicken only into serving plates and spoon the mayo-avocado sauce over.

Nutrition Info:

- Per Servings 4g Carbs, 24g Protein, 32g Fat, 398 Calories

Habanero Chicken Wings

Servings: 4 | Cooking Time: 65 Minutes

Ingredients:

- 2 pounds chicken wings
- Salt and black pepper, to taste
- 3 tbsp coconut aminos
- 2 tsp white vinegar
- 3 tbsp rice vinegar
- 3 tbsp stevia
- ¼ cup chives, chopped
- ½ tsp xanthan gum
- 5 dried habanero peppers, chopped

Directions:

1. Spread the chicken wings on a lined baking sheet, sprinkle with pepper and salt, set in an oven at 370ºF, and bake for 45 minutes. Put a small pan over medium heat, add in the white vinegar, coconut aminos, chives, stevia, rice vinegar, xanthan gum, and habanero peppers, bring the mixture to a boil, cook for 2 minutes, and remove from heat.
2. Dip the chicken wings into this sauce, lay them all on the baking sheet again, and bake for 10 more minutes. Serve warm.

Nutrition Info:

- Per Servings 2g Carbs, 26g Protein, 25g Fat, 416 Calories

Fried Chicken Breasts

Servings: 4 | Cooking Time: 20 Minutes

Ingredients:

- 2 chicken breasts, cut into strips
- 4 ounces pork rinds, crushed
- 2 cups coconut oil
- 16 ounces jarred pickle juice
- 2 eggs, whisked

Directions:

1. Using a bowl, combine the chicken breast pieces with pickle juice and refrigerate for 12 hours while covered. Set the eggs in a bowl, and pork rinds in a separate one. Dip the chicken pieces in the eggs, and then in pork rinds, and ensure they are well coated.
2. Set a pan over medium-high heat and warm oil, fry the chicken for 3 minutes on each side, remove to paper towels, drain the excess grease, and enjoy.

Nutrition Info:

- Per Servings 2.5g Carbs, 23g Protein, 16g Fat, 387 Calories

Chicken And Spinach

Servings: 8 | Cooking Time: 50 Minutes

Ingredients:

- 1-pound chicken breasts
- 2 jars commercial pasta sauce
- 2 cups baby spinach
- 1 onion chopped
- ¼ cup cheese
- 5 tbsps oil
- ½ cup water
- Pepper and salt to taste

Directions:

1. Place a heavy-bottomed pot on medium-high fire and heat pot for 2 minutes.
2. Add oil and swirl to coat sides and bottom of the pot. Heat oil for a minute.
3. Season chicken breasts with pepper and salt. Brown chicken for 4 minutes per side. Transfer to a chopping board and cut into ½-inch cubes.
4. In the same pot, sauté onions for 5 minutes. Add pasta sauce and season with pepper and salt. Stir in water and chicken breasts. Simmer pasta sauce for 30 minutes on low fire. Stir the bottom of the pot every now and then.
5. Mix spinach in a pot of sauce. Let it rest for 5 minutes.
6. Serve and enjoy with a sprinkle of cheese.

Nutrition Info:

- Per Servings 6.7g Carbs, 21.2g Protein, 15.6g Fat, 216 Calories

Sticky Cranberry Chicken Wings

Servings: 6 | Cooking Time: 50 Minutes

Ingredients:

- 2 lb chicken wings
- 4 tbsp unsweetened cranberry puree
- 2 tbsp olive oil
- Salt to taste
- Sweet chili sauce to taste
- Lemon juice from 1 lemon

Directions:

1. Preheat the oven (broiler side) to 400°F. Then, in a bowl, mix the cranberry puree, olive oil, salt, sweet chili sauce, and lemon juice. After, add in the wings and toss to coat.
2. Place the chicken under the broiler, and cook for 45 minutes, turning once halfway.
3. Remove the chicken after and serve warm with a cranberry and cheese dipping sauce.

Nutrition Info:

- Per Servings 1.6g Carbs, 17.6g Protein, 8.5g Fat, 152 Calories

Chicken Jambalaya

Servings: 6 | Cooking Time: 30 Minutes

Ingredients:

- ½ cup celery
- 3 chicken breast halves, skinless and boneless, chopped to bite-sized pieces
- 3 tbsp garlic, minced
- 3 whole tomatoes, chopped
- 1 tbsp Cajun seasoning
- 3 cups water
- 4 tbsps olive oil
- Pepper and salt to taste

Directions:

1. Place a pot on high fire and heat oil for 2 minutes.
2. Add chicken and garlic. Sauté for 5 minutes.
3. Add tomatoes, Cajun seasoning, salt, and pepper. Sauté for another 5 minutes.
4. Add water and simmer chicken for 10 minutes.
5. Stir in celery and continue cooking for another 5 minutes.
6. Adjust seasoning if needed.
7. Serve and enjoy.

Nutrition Info:

- Per Servings 4.8g Carbs, 35.0g Protein, 22.5g Fat, 419 Calories

Roasted Chicken With Herbs

Servings: 12 | Cooking Time: 50 Minutes

Ingredients:

- 1 whole chicken
- ½ tsp onion powder
- ½ tsp garlic powder
- Salt and black pepper, to taste
- 2 tbsp olive oil
- 1 tsp dry thyme
- 1 tsp dry rosemary
- 1 ½ cups chicken broth
- 2 tsp guar gum

Directions:

1. Rub the chicken with half of the oil, salt, rosemary, thyme, pepper, garlic powder, and onion powder. Place the rest of the oil into a baking dish, and add chicken. Place in the stock, and bake for 40 minutes. Remove the chicken to a platter, and set aside. Stir in the guar gum in a pan over medium heat, and cook until thickening. Place sauce over chicken to serve.

Nutrition Info:

- Per Servings 1.1g Carbs, 33g Protein, 15g Fat, 367 Calories

Pork, Beef & Lamb Recipes

Pork, Beef & Lamb Recipes

Habanero And Beef Balls

Servings: 6 | Cooking Time: 45 Minutes

Ingredients:

- 3 garlic cloves, minced
- 1 pound ground beef
- 1 small onion, chopped
- 2 habanero peppers, chopped
- 1 tsp dried thyme
- 2 tsp cilantro
- ½ tsp allspice
- 2 tsp cumin
- A pinch of ground cloves
- Salt and black pepper, to taste
- 2 tbsp butter
- 3 tbsp butter, melted
- 6 ounces cream cheese
- 1 tsp turmeric
- ¼ tsp stevia
- ½ tsp baking powder
- 1½ cups flax meal
- ½ cup coconut flour

Directions:

1. In a blender, mix onion with garlic, habaneros, and ½ cup water. Set a pan over medium heat, add in 2 tbsp butter and cook the beef for 3 minutes. Stir in the onion mixture, and cook for 2 minutes.
2. Stir in cilantro, cloves, salt, cumin, ½ teaspoon turmeric, thyme, allspice, and pepper, and cook for 3 minutes. In a bowl, combine the remaining turmeric, with coconut flour, stevia, flax meal, and baking powder. In a separate bowl, combine the 3 tbsp butter with the cream cheese.
3. Combine the 2 mixtures to obtain a dough. Form 12 balls from this mixture, set them on a parchment paper, and roll each into a circle. Split the beef mix on one-half of the dough circles, cover with the other half, seal edges, and lay on a lined sheet. Bake for 25 minutes in the oven at 350ºF.

Nutrition Info:

- Per Servings 8.3g Carbs, 27g Protein, 31g Fat, 455 Calories

Moroccan Style Beef Stew

Servings: 8 | Cooking Time: 45 Minutes

Ingredients:

- ½ cup sliced onions
- 4 tablespoons garam masala
- 2 pounds beef roast
- 5 tablespoons butter
- 1 large bell pepper, seeded and chopped
- 2 cups water
- Salt and pepper to taste
- 1 tablespoon oil

Directions:

1. Heat the oil in a heavy-bottomed pot over a high flame and sauté the onions for 10 minutes until lightly golden.
2. Stir in the garam masala and sear the beef roast on all sides.
3. Add remaining ingredients and bring to a boil.
4. Once boiling, lower fire to a simmer, cover, and cook for 30 minutes.
5. Serve and enjoy.

Nutrition Info:

- Per Servings 1.2g Carbs, 25.1g Protein, 30.8g Fat, 350 Calories

Rib Roast With Roasted Red Shallots And Garlic

Servings: 6 | Cooking Time: 55 Minutes

Ingredients:

- 5 lb rib roast, on the bone
- 3 heads garlic, cut in half
- 3 tbsp olive oil
- 6 shallots, peeled and halved
- 2 lemons, zested and juiced
- 3 tbsp mustard seeds
- 3 tbsp swerve
- Salt and black pepper to taste
- 3 tbsp thyme leaves

Directions:

1. Preheat the oven to 450°F. Place the garlic heads and shallots in the roasting dish, toss them with olive oil, and cook in the oven for 15 minutes. Pour the lemon juice on them and set aside. Score shallow crisscrosses patterns on the meat and set aside.
2. Mix the swerve, mustard seeds, thyme, salt, pepper, and lemon zest to make a rub; and apply it all over the beef with your hands particularly into the cuts. Place the beef on the shallots and garlic; cook it in the oven for 15 minutes. Reduce the heat to 400°F, cover the top of the dish with foil, and continue cooking for 5 minutes.
3. Once ready, remove the dish, and let the meat sit covered for 15 minutes before slicing. Use the beef pieces in salads or sandwiches.

Nutrition Info:

- Per Servings 2.5g Carbs, 58.4g Protein, 38.6g Fat, 556 Calories

Pancetta Sausage With Kale

Servings: 10 | Cooking Time: 25 Minutes

Ingredients:

- ½ gallon chicken broth
- A drizzle of olive oil
- 1 cup heavy cream
- 2 cups kale
- 6 pancetta slices, chopped
- 1 pound radishes, chopped
- 2 garlic cloves, minced
- Salt and black pepper, to taste
- A pinch of red pepper flakes
- 1 onion, chopped
- 1½ pounds hot pork sausage, chopped

Directions:

1. Set a pot over medium heat. Add in a drizzle of olive oil and warm. Stir in garlic, onion, pancetta, and sausage; cook for 5 minutes. Pour in broth, radishes, and kale, and simmer for 10 minutes.
2. Stir in the, salt, red pepper flakes, pepper, and heavy cream, and cook for about 5 minutes. Split among serving bowls and enjoy the meal.

Nutrition Info:

- Per Servings 5.4g Carbs, 21g Protein, 29g Fat, 386 Calories

Mustardy Pork Chops

Servings: 4 | Cooking Time: 15 Minutes

Ingredients:

- 4 pork loin chops
- 1 tsp Dijon mustard
- 1 tbsp soy sauce
- 1 tsp lemon juice
- 1 tbsp water
- Salt and black pepper, to taste
- 1 tbsp butter
- A bunch of scallions, chopped

Directions:

1. Using a bowl, combine the water with lemon juice, mustard and soy sauce. Set a pan over medium heat and warm butter, add in the pork chops, season with salt, and pepper, cook for 4 minutes, turn, and cook for additional 4 minutes. Remove the pork chops to a plate and keep warm.
2. In the same pan, pour in the mustard sauce, and simmer for 5 minutes. Spread this over pork, top with scallions, and enjoy.

Nutrition Info:

- Per Servings 1.2g Carbs, 38g Protein, 21.5g Fat, 382 Calories

Cherry-balsamic Sauced Beef

Servings: 4 | Cooking Time: 40 Minutes

Ingredients:

- 2-lbs London broil beef, sliced into 2-inch cubes
- 1/3 cup balsamic vinegar
- ½ cup dried cherries
- ½ teaspoon pepper
- 1 teaspoon salt
- 1 tablespoon canola oil
- ½ cup water

Directions:

1. Add all ingredients in a pot on high fire and bring to a boil.
2. Once boiling, lower fire to a simmer and cook for 35 minutes.
3. Adjust seasoning to taste.
4. Serve and enjoy.

Nutrition Info:

- Per Servings 4.6g Carbs, 82.2g Protein, 17.2g Fat, 525 Calories

Sweet Chipotle Grilled Ribs

Servings: 4 | Cooking Time: 32 Minutes

Ingredients:

- 2 tbsp erythritol
- Pink salt and black pepper to taste
- 1 tbsp olive oil
- 3 tsp chipotle powder
- 1 tsp garlic powder
- 1 lb spare ribs
- 4 tbsp sugar-free BBQ sauce + extra for serving

Directions:

1. Mix the erythritol, salt, pepper, oil, chipotle, and garlic powder. Brush on the meaty sides of the ribs and wrap in foil. Sit for 30 minutes to marinate.
2. Preheat oven to 400°F, place wrapped ribs on a baking sheet, and cook for 40 minutes to be cooked through. Remove ribs and aluminium foil, brush with BBQ sauce, and brown under the broiler for 10 minutes on both sides. Slice and serve with extra BBQ sauce and lettuce tomato salad.

Nutrition Info:

- Per Servings 3g Carbs, 21g Protein, 33g Fat, 395 Calories

Bacon Stew With Cauliflower

Servings: 6 | Cooking Time: 40 Minutes

Ingredients:

- 8 ounces mozzarella cheese, grated
- 2 cups chicken broth
- ½ tsp garlic powder
- ½ tsp onion powder
- Salt and black pepper, to taste
- 4 garlic cloves, minced
- ¼ cup heavy cream
- 3 cups bacon, chopped
- 1 head cauliflower, cut into florets

Directions:

1. In a pot, combine the bacon with broth, cauliflower, salt, heavy cream, pepper, garlic powder, cheese, onion powder, and garlic, and cook for 35 minutes, share into serving plates, and enjoy.

Nutrition Info:

- Per Servings 6g Carbs, 33g Protein, 25g Fat, 380 Calories

Jalapeno Beef Pot Roasted

Servings: 4 | Cooking Time: 1 Hour 25 Minutes

Ingredients:

- 3½ pounds beef roast
- 4 ounces mushrooms, sliced
- 12 ounces beef stock
- 1 ounce onion soup mix
- ½ cup Italian dressing
- 2 jalapeños, shredded

Directions:

1. Using a bowl, combine the stock with the Italian dressing and onion soup mixture. Place the beef roast in a pan, stir in the stock mixture, mushrooms, and jalapeños; cover with aluminum foil.
2. Set in the oven at 300°F, and bake for 1 hour. Take out the foil and continue baking for 15 minutes. Allow the roast to cool, slice, and serve alongside a topping of the gravy.

Nutrition Info:

- Per Servings 3.2g Carbs, 87g Protein, 46g Fat, 745 Calories

Classic Meatloaf

Servings: 3 | Cooking Time: 40 Mins

Directions:

1. Preheat the oven to 325 degrees F.
2. Place the celery, onion and garlic in a food processor.
3. Place the minced vegetables into a large mixing bowl, and mix in ground chuck, Italian herbs, salt, black pepper, and cayenne pepper.
4. Whisk in the almond flour, stirring well, about 1 minute.
5. Sprinkle the olive oil into a baking dish and place meat into the dish. Shape the ball into a loaf. Bake in the preheated oven for 15 minutes.
6. In a small bowl, mix together ketchup, Dijon mustard, and hot sauce, stirring well to combined.
7. Bake the meatloaf for 30 to 40 more minutes at least 160 degrees F.

Nutrition Info:

- Per Servings 10.8g Carbs, 21.6g Protein, 19g Fat, 300 Calories

Pork Burgers With Caramelized Onion Rings

Servings: 6 | Cooking Time: 20 Minutes

Ingredients:

- 2 lb ground pork
- Pink salt and chili pepper to taste
- 3 tbsp olive oil
- 1 tbsp butter
- 1 white onion, sliced into rings
- 1 tbsp balsamic vinegar
- 3 drops liquid stevia
- 6 low carb burger buns, halved
- 2 firm tomatoes, sliced into rings

Directions:

1. Combine the pork, salt and chili pepper in a bowl and mold out 6 patties.
2. Heat the olive oil in a skillet over medium heat and fry the patties for 4 to 5 minutes on each side until golden brown on the outside. Remove onto a plate and sit for 3 minutes.
3. Meanwhile, melt butter in a skillet over medium heat, sauté the onions for 2 minutes to be soft, and stir in the balsamic vinegar and liquid stevia.
4. Cook for 30 seconds stirring once or twice until caramelized. In each bun, place a patty, top with some onion rings and 2 tomato rings. Serve the burgers with cheddar cheese dip.

Nutrition Info:

- Per Servings 7.6g Carbs, 26g Protein, 32g Fat, 445 Calories

North African Lamb

Servings: 4 | Cooking Time: 25 Minutes

Ingredients:

- 2 tsp paprika
- 2 garlic cloves, minced
- 2 tsp dried oregano
- 2 tbsp sumac
- 12 lamb cutlets
- ¼ cup sesame oil
- 2 tbsp water
- 2 tsp cumin
- 4 carrots, sliced
- ¼ cup fresh parsley, chopped
- 2 tsp harissa paste
- 1 tbsp red wine vinegar
- Salt and black pepper, to taste
- 2 tbsp black olives, sliced
- 2 cucumbers, sliced thin

Directions:

1. Using a bowl, combine the cutlets with the paprika, oregano, pepper, water, half of the oil, sumac, garlic, and salt, and rub well. Add the carrots in a pot, cover with the water, bring to a boil over medium-high heat, cook for 2 minutes then drain before placing them in a salad bowl.
2. Place the cucumbers and olives to the carrots. In another bowl, combine the harissa with the rest of the oil, a splash of water, parsley, vinegar, and cumin. Place this to the carrots mixture, season with pepper and salt, and toss well to coat. Heat a grill over medium heat and arrange the lamb cutlets on it, grill each side for 3 minutes, and split among separate plates. Serve alongside the carrot salad.

Nutrition Info:

- Per Servings 4g Carbs, 34g Protein, 32g Fat, 445 Calories

Greek Pork With Olives

Servings: 4 | Cooking Time: 45 Minutes

Ingredients:

- 4 pork chops, bone-in
- Salt and ground black pepper, to taste
- 1 tsp dried rosemary
- 3 garlic cloves, peeled and minced
- ½ cup kalamata olives, pitted and sliced
- 2 tbsp olive oil
- ¼ cup vegetable broth

Directions:

1. Season pork chops with pepper and salt, and add in a roasting pan. Stir in the garlic, olives, olive oil, broth, and rosemary, set in the oven at 425°F, and bake for 10 minutes. Reduce heat to 350°F and roast for 25 minutes. Slice the pork, split among plates, and sprinkle with pan juices all over.

Nutrition Info:

- Per Servings 2.2g Carbs, 36g Protein, 25.2g Fat, 415 Calories

Bistro Beef Tenderloin

Servings: 7 | Cooking Time: 45 Minutes

Ingredients:

- 1 3-pound beef tenderloin, trimmed of fat
- 2/3 cup chopped mixed herbs
- 2 tablespoons Dijon mustard
- 5 tablespoons extra virgin olive oil
- ½ teaspoon ground black pepper
- ½ tsp salt

Directions:

1. Preheat the oven to 400F.
2. Secure the beef tenderloin with a string in three places so that it does not flatten while roasting.
3. Place the beef tenderloin in a dish and rub onto the meat the olive oil, black pepper, salt, and mixed herb.
4. Place on a roasting pan and cook in the oven for 45 minutes.
5. Roast until the thermometer inserted into the thickest part of the meat until it registers 1400F for medium rare.
6. Place the tenderloin on a chopping board and remove the string. Slice into 1-inch thick slices and brush with Dijon mustard.

Nutrition Info:

- Per Servings 0.6g Carbs, 59.0g Protein, 22.0g Fat, 440 Calories

Beef Stovies

Servings: 4 | Cooking Time: 60 Minutes

Ingredients:

- 1 lb ground beef
- 1 large onion, chopped
- 6 parsnips, peeled and chopped
- 1 large carrot, chopped
- 1 tbsp olive oil
- 1 clove garlic, minced
- Salt and black pepper to taste
- 1 cup chicken broth
- ¼ tsp allspice
- 2 tsp rosemary leaves
- 1 tbsp sugar-free Worcestershire sauce
- ½ small cabbage, shredded

Directions:

1. Heat the oil in a skillet over medium heat and cook the beef for 4 minutes. Season with salt and pepper, and occasionally stir while breaking the lumps in it.
2. Add the onion, garlic, carrots, rosemary, and parsnips. Stir and cook for a minute, and pour the chicken broth, allspice, and Worcestershire sauce in it. Stir the mixture and cook the ingredients on low heat for 40 minutes.
3. Stir in the cabbage, season with salt and pepper, and cook the ingredients further for 2 minutes. After, turn the heat off, plate the stovies, and serve with wilted spinach and collards.

Nutrition Info:

- Per Servings 3g Carbs, 14g Protein, 18g Fat, 316 Calories

Pork Lettuce Cups

Servings: 6 | Cooking Time: 20 Minutes

Ingredients:

- 2 lb ground pork
- 1 tbsp ginger- garlic paste
- Pink salt and chili pepper to taste
- 1 tsp ghee
- 1 head Iceberg lettuce
- 2 sprigs green onion, chopped
- 1 red bell pepper, seeded and chopped
- ½ cucumber, finely chopped

Directions:

1. Put the pork with ginger-garlic paste, salt, and chili pepper seasoning in a saucepan. Cook for 10 minutes over medium heat while breaking any lumps until the pork is no longer pink. Drain liquid and add the ghee, melt and brown the meat for 4 minutes, continuously stirring. Turn the heat off.
2. Pat the lettuce dry with paper towel and in each leaf, spoon two to three tablespoons of pork, top with green onions, bell pepper, and cucumber. Serve with soy drizzling sauce.

Nutrition Info:

- Per Servings 1g Carbs, 19g Protein, 24.3g Fat, 311 Calories

Warm Rump Steak Salad

Servings: 4 | Cooking Time: 40 Minutes

Ingredients:

- ½ lb rump steak, excess fat trimmed
- 3 green onions, sliced
- 3 tomatoes, sliced
- 1 cup green beans, steamed and sliced
- 2 kohlrabi, peeled and chopped
- ½ cup water
- 2 cups mixed salad greens
- Salt and black pepper to season
- Salad Dressing
- 2 tsp Dijon mustard
- 1 tsp erythritol
- Salt and black pepper to taste
- 3 tbsp olive oil + extra for drizzling
- 1 tbsp red wine vinegar

Directions:

1. Preheat the oven to 400ºF. Place the kohlrabi on a baking sheet, drizzle with olive oil and bake in the oven for 25 minutes. After cooking, remove, and set aside to cool.
2. In a bowl, mix the Dijon mustard, erythritol, salt, pepper, vinegar, and olive oil. Set aside.
3. Then, preheat a grill pan over high heat while you season the meat with salt and pepper. Place the steak in the pan and brown on both sides for 4 minutes each. Remove to rest on a chopping board for 4 more minutes before slicing thinly.
4. In a shallow salad bowl, add the green onions, tomatoes, green beans, kohlrabi, salad greens, and steak slices. Drizzle the dressing over and toss with two spoons. Serve the rump steak salad warm with chunks of low carb bread.

Nutrition Info:

- Per Servings 4g Carbs, 28g Protein, 19g Fat, 325 Calories

Zucchini Boats With Beef And Pimiento Rojo

Servings: 4 | Cooking Time: 30 Minutes

Ingredients:

- 4 zucchinis
- 2 tbsp olive oil
- 1 ½ lb ground beef
- 1 medium red onion, chopped
- 2 tbsp chopped pimiento
- Pink salt and black pepper to taste
- 1 cup grated yellow cheddar cheese

Directions:

1. Preheat oven to 350ºF.
2. Lay the zucchinis on a flat surface, trim off the ends and cut in half lengthwise. Scoop out pulp from each half with a spoon to make shells. Chop the pulp.
3. Heat oil in a skillet; add the ground beef, red onion, pimiento, and zucchini pulp, and season with salt and black pepper. Cook for 6 minutes while stirring to break up lumps until beef is no longer pink. Turn the heat off. Spoon the beef into the boats and sprinkle with cheddar cheese.
4. Place on a greased baking sheet and cook to melt the cheese for 15 minutes until zucchini boats are tender. Take out, cool for 2 minutes, and serve warm with a mixed green salad.

Nutrition Info:

- Per Servings 7g Carbs, 18g Protein, 24g Fat, 335 Calories

Homemade Classic Beef Burgers

Servings: 4 | Cooking Time: 15 Minutes

Ingredients:

- 1 pound ground beef
- ½ tsp onion powder
- ½ tsp garlic powder
- 2 tbsp ghee
- 1 tsp Dijon mustard
- 4 low carb buns, halved
- ¼ cup mayonnaise
- 1 tsp sriracha
- 4 tbsp cabbage slaw

Directions:

1. Mix together the beef, onion, garlic powder, mustard, salt, and black pepper; create 4 burgers. Melt the ghee in a skillet and cook the burgers for about 3 minutes per side. Serve in buns topped with mayo, sriracha, and slaw.

Nutrition Info:

- Per Servings 7.9g Carbs, 39g Protein, 55g Fat, 664 Calories

Beef Meatballs With Onion Sauce

Servings: 5 | Cooking Time: 35 Minutes

Ingredients:

- 2 pounds ground beef
- Salt and black pepper, to taste
- ½ tsp garlic powder
- 1 ¼ tbsp coconut aminos
- 1 cup beef stock
- ¾ cup almond flour
- 1 tbsp fresh parsley, chopped
- 1 tbsp dried onion flakes
- 1 onion, sliced
- 2 tbsp butter
- ¼ cup sour cream

Directions:

1. Using a bowl, combine the beef with salt, garlic powder, almond flour, onion flakes, parsley, 1 tablespoon coconut aminos, black pepper, ¼ cup of beef stock. Form 6 patties, place them on a baking sheet, put in the oven at 370ºF, and bake for 18 minutes.
2. Set a pan with the butter over medium heat, stir in the onion, and cook for 3 minutes. Stir in the remaining beef stock, sour cream, and remaining coconut aminos, and bring to a simmer.
3. Remove from heat, adjust the seasoning with black pepper and salt. Serve the meatballs topped with onion sauce.

Nutrition Info:

- Per Servings 6g Carbs, 32g Protein, 23g Fat, 435 Calories

Grilled Sirloin Steak With Sauce Diane

Servings: 6 | Cooking Time: 25 Minutes

Ingredients:

- Sirloin Steak
- 1 ½ lb sirloin steak
- Salt and black pepper to taste
- 1 tsp olive oil
- Sauce Diane
- 1 tbsp olive oil
- 1 clove garlic, minced
- 1 cup sliced porcini mushrooms
- 1 small onion, finely diced
- 2 tbsp butter
- 1 tbsp Dijon mustard
- 2 tbsp sugar-free Worcestershire sauce
- ¼ cup whiskey
- 2 cups double cream
- Salt and black pepper to taste

Directions:

1. Preheat the grill pan over high heat and as it heats, brush the steak with oil, sprinkle with salt and pepper, and rub the seasoning into the meat with your hands.
2. Cook the steak in the pan for 4 minutes on each side for medium rare and transfer to a chopping board to rest for 4 minutes before slicing. (Reserve the juice in the pan to season the sauce).
3. Heat the oil in a frying pan over medium heat and sauté the onion for 3 minutes. Add the butter, garlic, and mushrooms, and cook for 2 minutes.
4. Add the Worcestershire sauce, the reserved juice, and mustard. Stir and cook for 1 minute. Pour in the whiskey and cook further 1 minute until the sauce reduces by half. Swirl the pan and add the cream. Let it simmer to thicken for about 3 minutes. Adjust the taste with salt and pepper. Spoon the sauce over the steaks slices and serve with a side of celeriac mash.

Nutrition Info:

- Per Servings 2.9g Carbs, 36g Protein, 17g Fat, 434 Calories

White Wine Lamb Chops

Servings: 6 | Cooking Time: 1 Hour And 25 Minutes

Ingredients:

- 6 lamb chops
- 1 tbsp sage
- 1 tsp thyme
- 1 onion, sliced
- 3 garlic cloves, minced
- 2 tbsp olive oil
- ½ cup white wine
- Salt and black pepper, to taste

Directions:

1. Heat the olive oil in a pan. Add onion and garlic and cook for 3 minutes, until soft. Rub the sage and thyme over the lamb chops. Cook the lamb for about 3 minutes per side. Set aside.
2. Pour the white wine and 1 cup of water into the pan, bring the mixture to a boil. Cook until the liquid is reduced by half. Add the chops in the pan, reduce the heat, and let simmer for 1 hour.

Nutrition Info:

- Per Servings 4.3g Carbs, 16g Protein, 30g Fat, 397 Calories

Creamy Pork Chops

Servings: 3 | Cooking Time: 50 Minutes

Ingredients:

- 8 ounces mushrooms, sliced
- 1 tsp garlic powder
- 1 onion, peeled and chopped
- 1 cup heavy cream
- 3 pork chops, boneless
- 1 tsp ground nutmeg
- ¼ cup coconut oil

Directions:

1. Set a pan over medium heat and warm the oil, add in the onions and mushrooms, and cook for 4 minutes. Stir in the pork chops, season with garlic powder, and nutmeg, and sear until browned.
2. Put the pan in the oven at 350ºF, and bake for 30 minutes. Remove pork chops to bowls and maintain warm. Place the pan over medium heat, pour in the heavy cream and vinegar over the mushrooms mixture, and cook for 5 minutes; remove from heat. Sprinkle sauce over pork chops and enjoy.

Nutrition Info:

- Per Servings 6.8g Carbs, 42g Protein, 40g Fat, 612 Calories

Beef And Cabbage With Spice Packet

Servings: 5 | Cooking Time: 1h 20mins

Ingredients:

- 3 pounds corned beef brisket with spice packet
- 1 large head cabbage, cut into small wedges
- 1 cup diced onion
- 3 cups water
- 2 cups beef broth

Directions:

1. Place corned beef in large pot and cover with water. Add the spice packet to the corned beef.
2. Cover the pot and bring to a boil, simmering for 50 minutes.
3. Add the cabbage and onion, cook until the vegetables are almost tender.
4. Remove beef and cool for 15 minutes.
5. Transfer vegetables into a bowl and cover. Add as much broth as you want. Slice meat across the grain. Serve and enjoy.

Nutrition Info:

- Per Servings 11g Carbs, 21g Protein, 23.7g Fat, 341 Calories

Pork Casserole

Servings: 4 | Cooking Time: 38 Minutes

Ingredients:

- 1 lb ground pork
- 1 large yellow squash, thinly sliced
- Salt and black pepper to taste
- 1 clove garlic, minced
- 4 green onions, chopped
- 1 cup chopped cremini mushrooms
- 1 can diced tomatoes
- ½ cup pork rinds, crushed
- ¼ cup chopped parsley
- 1 cup cottage cheese
- 1 cup Mexican cheese blend
- 3 tbsp olive oil
- ⅓ cup water

Directions:

1. Preheat the oven to 370ºF.
2. Heat the olive oil in a skillet over medium heat, add the pork, season it with salt and pepper, and cook for 3 minutes or until no longer pink. Stir occasionally while breaking any lumps apart.
3. Add the garlic, half of the green onions, mushrooms, and 2 tablespoons of pork rinds. Continue cooking for 3 minutes. Stir in the tomatoes, half of the parsley, and water. Cook further for 3 minutes, and then turn the heat off.
4. Mix the remaining parsley, cottage cheese, and Mexican cheese blend. Set aside. Sprinkle the bottom of a baking dish with 3 tablespoons of pork rinds; top with half of the squash and a season of salt, 2/3 of the pork mixture, and the cheese mixture. Repeat the layering process a second time to exhaust the ingredients.
5. Cover the baking dish with foil and put in the oven to bake for 20 minutes. After, remove the foil and brown the top of the casserole with the broiler side of the oven for 2 minutes. Remove the dish when ready and serve the casserole warm.

Nutrition Info:

- Per Servings 2.7g Carbs, 36.5g Protein, 29g Fat, 495 Calories

Fish And Seafood Recipes

Yummy Shrimp Fried Rice

Servings: 6 | Cooking Time: 20 Minutes

Ingredients:
- 4 tablespoons butter, divided
- 4 large eggs, lightly beaten
- 3 cups shredded cauliflower
- 1-pound uncooked medium shrimp, peeled and deveined
- 1/2 teaspoon salt
- 1/4 teaspoon pepper

Directions:

1. In a large skillet, melt 1 tablespoon butter over medium-high heat.
2. Pour eggs into skillet. As eggs set, lift edges, letting uncooked portion flow underneath. Remove eggs and keep warm.
3. Melt remaining butter in the skillet. Add the cauliflower, and shrimp; cook and stir for 5 minutes or until shrimp turn pink.
4. Meanwhile, chop eggs into small pieces. Return eggs to the pan; sprinkle with salt and pepper. Cook until heated through, stirring occasionally. Sprinkle with bacon if desired.

Nutrition Info:
- Per Servings 3.3g Carbs, 13g Protein, 11g Fat, 172 Calories

Air Fryer Seasoned Salmon Fillets

Servings: 4 | Cooking Time: 10 Mins

Ingredients:
- 2 lbs. salmon fillets
- 1 tsp. stevia
- 2 tbsp. whole grain mustard
- 1 clove of garlic, minced
- 1/2 tsp. thyme leaves
- 2 tsp. extra-virgin olive oil
- Cooking spray
- Salt and black pepper to taste

Directions:

1. Preheat your Air Fryer to 390 degrees F.
2. Season salmon fillets with salt and pepper.
3. Add together the mustard, garlic, stevia, thyme, and oil in a bowl, stir to combined well. Rub the seasoning mixture on top of salmon fillets.
4. Spray the Air Fryer basket with cooking spray and cook seasoned fillets for 10 minutes until crispy. Let it cool before serving.

Nutrition Info:
- Per Servings 14g Carbs, 18g Protein, 10g Fat, 238 Calories

Asian-style Fish Salad

Serves: 2 | Cooking Time: 15 Minutes

Ingredients:

- Salad:
- 1/4 cup water
- 1/4 cup Sauvignon Blanc
- 1/2 pound salmon fillets
- 1 cup Chinese cabbage, sliced
- 1 tomato, sliced
- 2 radishes, sliced
- 1 bell pepper, sliced
- 1 medium-sized white onion, sliced
- Salad Dressing:
- 1/2 teaspoon fresh garlic, minced
- 1 fresh chili pepper, seeded and minced
- 1/2 teaspoon fresh ginger, peeled and grated
- 2 tablespoons fresh lime juice
- 1 tablespoon sesame oil
- 1 tablespoon tamari sauce
- 1 teaspoon xylitol
- 1 tablespoon fresh mint, roughly chopped
- Sea salt and freshly ground black pepper, to taste

Directions:

1. Place the water and Sauvignon Blanc in a sauté pan; bring to a simmer over moderate heat.
2. Place the salmon fillets, skin-side down in the pan and cover with the lid. Cook for 5 to 8 minutes or to your desired doneness; do not overcook the salmon; reserve.
3. Place the Chinese cabbage, tomato, radishes, bell pepper, and onion in a serving bowl.
4. Prepare the salad dressing by whisking all ingredients. Dress your salad, top with the salmon fillets and serve immediately!

Nutrition Info:

- Per Serves4.9g Carbs; 24.4g Protein; 15.1g Fat; 277 Calories

Simply Steamed Alaskan Cod

Servings: 2 | Cooking Time: 15 Minutes

Ingredients:

- 1-lb fillet wild Alaskan Cod
- 1 cup cherry tomatoes, halved
- 1 tbsp balsamic vinegar
- 1 tbsp fresh basil chopped
- Salt and pepper to taste
- 5 tbsp olive oil

Directions:

1. In a heat-proof dish that fits inside the saucepan, add all ingredients except for basil. Mix well.
2. Place a large saucepan on the medium-high fire. Place a trivet inside the saucepan and fill pan halfway with water. Cover and bring to a boil.
3. Cover dish with foil and place on a trivet.
4. Cover pan and steam for 10 minutes. Let it rest in pan for another 5 minutes.
5. Serve and enjoy topped with fresh basil.

Nutrition Info:

- Per Servings 4.2g Carbs, 41.0g Protein, 36.6g Fat, 495.2 Calories

Cod In Garlic Butter Sauce

Servings: 6 | Cooking Time: 20 Minutes

Ingredients:

- 2 tsp olive oil
- 6 Alaska cod fillets
- Salt and black pepper to taste
- 4 tbsp salted butter
- 4 cloves garlic, minced
- ⅓ cup lemon juice
- 3 tbsp white wine
- 2 tbsp chopped chives

Directions:

1. Heat the oil in a skillet over medium heat and season the cod with salt and black pepper. Fry the fillets in the oil for 4 minutes on one side, flip and cook for 1 minute. Take out, plate, and set aside.
2. In another skillet over low heat, melt the butter and sauté the garlic for 3 minutes. Add the lemon juice, wine, and chives. Season with salt, black pepper, and cook for 3 minutes until the wine slightly reduces. Put the fish in the skillet, spoon sauce over, cook for 30 seconds and turn the heat off.
3. Divide fish into 6 plates, top with sauce, and serve with buttered green beans.

Nutrition Info:

- Per Servings 2.3g Carbs, 20g Protein, 17.3g Fat, 264 Calories

Red Curry Halibut

Servings: 4 | Cooking Time: 15 Minutes

Ingredients:

- 4 halibut fillets, skin removed
- 1 cup chopped tomatoes
- 3 green curry leaves
- 2 tbsp. chopped cilantro
- 1 tbsp. lime juice, freshly squeezed
- 3 tbsp olive oil
- Pepper and salt to taste

Directions:

1. Place a trivet in a large saucepan and pour a cup or two of water into the pan. Bring to a boil.
2. Place halibut in a heatproof dish that fits inside the saucepan. Season halibut with pepper and salt. Drizzle with olive oil. Sprinkle chopped tomatoes, curry leaves, chopped cilantro, and lime juice.
3. Seal dish with foil. Place the dish on the trivet inside the saucepan. Cover and steam for 15 minutes.
4. Serve and enjoy.

Nutrition Info:

- Per Servings 1.8g Carbs, 76.1g Protein, 15.5g Fat, 429 Calories

Steamed Greek Snapper

Servings: 12 | Cooking Time: 15 Minutes

Ingredients:

- 6 tbsp. olive oil
- 1 clove of garlic, minced
- 2 tbsp. Greek yogurt
- 12 snapper fillets
- Salt and pepper to taste

Directions:

1. In a small bowl, combine the olive oil, garlic, and Greek yogurt. Season with salt and pepper to taste.
2. Place a trivet in a large saucepan and pour a cup or two of water into the pan. Bring to a boil.
3. Place snapper in a heatproof dish that fits inside a saucepan. If needed, cook in batches. Season snapper with pepper and salt and drizzle with olive oil. Slather with yogurt mixture.
4. Seal dish with foil. Place the dish on the trivet inside the saucepan. Cover and steam for 15 minutes.
5. Serve and enjoy.

Nutrition Info:

- Per Servings 0.4g Carbs, 44.8g Protein, 9.8g Fat, 280 Calories

Boiled Garlic Clams

Servings: 6 | Cooking Time: 10 Minutes

Ingredients:

- 3 tbsp butter
- 6 cloves of garlic
- 50 small clams in the shell, scrubbed
- ½ cup fresh parsley, chopped
- 4 tbsp. extra virgin olive oil
- 1 cup water
- Salt and pepper to taste

Directions:

1. Heat the olive oil and butter in a large pot placed on medium-high fire for a minute.
2. Stir in the garlic and cook until fragrant and slightly browned.
3. Stir in the clams, water, and parsley. Season with salt and pepper to taste.
4. Cover and cook for 5 minutes or until clams have opened.
5. Discard unopened clams and serve.

Nutrition Info:

- Per Servings 0.9g Carbs, 11.3g Protein, 12.8g Fat, 159 Calories

Mustard-crusted Salmon

Servings: 4 | Cooking Time: 15 Minutes

Ingredients:

- 1 ¼ lb. salmon fillets, cut into 4 portions
- 2 tsp. lemon juice
- 2 tbsp. stone-ground mustard
- Lemon wedges, for garnish
- 4 tbsp olive oil
- Salt and pepper to taste

Directions:

1. Place a trivet in a large saucepan and pour a cup of water into the pan. Bring to a boil.
2. Place salmon in a heatproof dish that fits inside saucepan and drizzle with olive oil. Season the salmon fillets with salt, pepper, and lemon juice. Sprinkle with mustard on top and garnish with lemon wedges on top. Seal dish with foil.
3. Place the dish on the trivet inside the saucepan. Cover and steam for 15 minutes.
4. Serve and enjoy.

Nutrition Info:

- Per Servings 2.9g Carbs, 29g Protein, 24.8g Fat, 360 Calories

Seasoned Salmon With Parmesan

Servings: 4 | Cooking Time: 20 Mins

Ingredients:

- 2 lbs. salmon fillet
- 3 minced garlic cloves
- ¼ cup. chopped parsley
- ½ cup. grated parmesan cheese
- Salt and pepper to taste

Directions:

1. Preheat oven to 425 degrees F. Line a baking sheet with parchment paper.
2. Lay salmon fillets on the lined baking sheet, season with salt and pepper to taste.
3. Bake for 10 minutes. Remove from the oven and sprinkle with garlic, parmesan and parsley.
4. Place in the oven to cook for 5 more minutes. Transfer to plates before serving.

Nutrition Info:

- Per Servings 0.6g Carbs, 25g Protein, 12g Fat, 210 Calories

Avocado & Cauliflower Salad With Prawns

Serves:6 | Cooking Time: 30 Minutes

Ingredients:

- 1 cauliflower head, florets only
- 1 lb medium-sized prawns
- ¼ cup + 1 tbsp olive oil
- 1 avocado, chopped
- 3 tbsp chopped dill
- ¼ cup lemon juice
- 2 tbsp lemon zest

Directions:

1. Heat 1 tbsp olive oil in a skillet and cook the prawns for 8-10 minutes. Microwave cauliflower for 5 minutes. Place prawns, cauliflower, and avocado in a large bowl. Whisk together the remaining olive oil, lemon zest, juice, dill, and some salt and pepper, in another bowl. Pour the dressing over, toss to combine and serve immediately.

Nutrition Info:

- Per Serves 5g Carbs ; 15g Protein, 17g Fat; 214 Calories

Cedar Salmon With Green Onion

Servings: 5 | Cooking Time: 20 Mins

Ingredients:

- 3 untreated cedar planks
- 1/4 cup. chopped green onions
- 1 tablespoon. grated fresh ginger root
- 1 teaspoon. minced garlic
- 2 salmon fillets, skin removed
- 1/3 cup. olive oil
- 1/3 cup. mayo
- 1 1/2 tablespoons. rice vinegar

Directions:

1. Soak cedar planks in warm water for 1 hour more.
2. Whisk olive oil, rice vinegar, mayo, green onions, ginger, and garlic in a bowl. Marinade salmon fillets to coat completely. Cover the bowl with plastic wrap and marinate for 15 to 60 minutes.
3. Preheat an outdoor grill over medium heat. Lay planks on the center of hot grate Place the salmon fillets onto the planks and remove the marinade. Cover the grill and cook until cooked through, about 20 minutes, or until salmon is done to your liking. Serve the salmon on a platter right off the planks.

Nutrition Info:

- Per Servings 10g Carbs, 18g Protein, 27g Fat, 355 Calories

Baked Salmon With Pistachio Crust

Serves:4 | Cooking Time: 35 Minutes

Ingredients:

- 4 salmon fillets
- ¼ cup mayonnaise
- ½ cup ground pistachios
- 1 chopped shallot
- 2 tsp lemon zest
- 1 tbsp olive oil
- A pinch of pepper
- 1 cup heavy cream

Directions:

1. Preheat oven to 375 °F. Brush salmon with mayo and season with salt and pepper. Coat with pistachios. Place in a lined baking dish and bake for 15 minutes. Heat the olive oil in a saucepan and sauté shallot for 3 minutes. Stir in heavy cream and lemon zest. Bring to a boil and cook until thickened. Serve salmon with the sauce.

Nutrition Info:

- Per Serves 6g Carbs; 34g Protein; 47g Fat ; 563 Calories

Baked Calamari And Shrimp

Serves: 1 | Cooking Time: 20 Minutes

Ingredients:

- 8 ounces calamari, cut in medium rings
- 7 ounces shrimp, peeled and deveined
- 1 eggs
- 3 tablespoons coconut flour
- 1 tablespoon coconut oil
- 2 tablespoons avocado, chopped
- 1 teaspoon tomato paste
- 1 tablespoon mayonnaise
- A splash of Worcestershire sauce
- 1 teaspoon lemon juice
- 2 lemon slices
- Salt and black pepper to the taste
- ½ teaspoon turmeric

Directions:

1. In a bowl, whisk egg with coconut oil.
2. Add calamari rings and shrimp and toss to coat.
3. In another bowl, mix flour with salt, pepper and turmeric and stir.
4. Dredge calamari and shrimp in this mix, place everything on a lined baking sheet, introduce in the oven at 400 °F and bake for 10 minutes.
5. Flip calamari and shrimp and bake for 10 minutes more.
6. Meanwhile, in a bowl, mix avocado with mayo and tomato paste and mash using a fork.
7. Add Worcestershire sauce, lemon juice, salt and pepper and stir well.
8. Divide baked calamari and shrimp on plates and serve with the sauce and lemon juice on the side.
9. Enjoy!

Nutrition Info:

- 10 carbs; 34 protein; 23 fat; 368 calories

Lemon Marinated Salmon With Spices

Servings: 2 | Cooking Time: 15 Minutes

Ingredients:

- 2 tablespoons. lemon juice
- 1 tablespoon. yellow miso paste
- 2 teaspoons. Dijon mustard
- 1 pinch cayenne pepper and sea salt to taste
- 2 center-cut salmon fillets, boned; skin on
- 1 1/2 tablespoons mayonnaise
- 1 tablespoon ground black pepper

Directions:

1. In a bowl, combine lemon juice with black pepper. Stir in mayonnaise, miso paste, Dijon mustard, and cayenne pepper, mix well. Pour over salmon fillets, reserve about a tablespoon marinade. Cover and marinate the fish in the refrigerator for 30 minutes.
2. Preheat oven to 450 degrees F. Line a baking sheet with parchment paper.
3. Lay fillets on the prepared baking sheet. Rub the reserved lemon-pepper marinade on fillets. Then season with cayenne pepper and sea salt to taste.
4. Bake in the oven for 10 to 15 minutes until cooked through.

Nutrition Info:

- Per Servings 7.1g Carbs, 20g Protein, 28.1g Fat, 361 Calories

Steamed Ginger Scallion Fish

Cooking Time: 15 Minutes

Ingredients:

- 3 tablespoons soy sauce, low sodium
- 2 tablespoons rice wine
- 1 teaspoon minced ginger
- 1 teaspoon garlic
- 1-pound firm white fish
- Pepper to taste
- 4 tbsps sesame oil

Directions:

1. In a heat-proof dish that fits inside the saucepan, add all ingredients. Mix well.
2. Place a large saucepan on the medium-high fire. Place a trivet inside the saucepan and fill the pan halfway with water. Cover and bring to a boil.
3. Cover dish with foil and place on a trivet.
4. Cover pan and steam for 10 minutes. Let it rest in pan for another 5 minutes.
5. Serve and enjoy.

Nutrition Info:

- Per Servings 5.5g Carbs, 44.9g Protein, 23.1g Fat, 409.5 Calories

Shrimp And Cauliflower Jambalaya

Servings: 4 | Cooking Time: 15 Minutes

Ingredients:

- 2 cloves garlic, peeled and minced
- 1 head cauliflower, grated
- 1 cup chopped tomatoes
- 8 oz. raw shrimp, peeled and deveined
- 1 tbsp Cajun seasoning
- Salt and pepper
- 4 tbsp coconut oil
- 1 tbsp water

Directions:

1. On medium-high fire, heat a nonstick saucepan for 2 minutes. Add oil to a pan and swirl to coat bottom and sides. Heat oil for a minute.
2. Add garlic and sauté for a minute. Stir in tomatoes and stir fry for 5 minutes. Add water and deglaze the pan.
3. Add remaining ingredients. Season generously with pepper.
4. Increase fire to high and stir fry for 3 minutes.
5. Lower fire to low, cover, and cook for 5 minutes.
6. Serve and enjoy.

Nutrition Info:

- Per Servings 7.8g Carbs, 21.4g Protein, 22.25g Fat, 314 Calories

Shrimp Stuffed Zucchini

Servings: 4 | Cooking Time: 56 Minutes

Ingredients:

- 4 medium zucchinis
- 1 lb small shrimp, peeled, deveined
- 1 tbsp minced onion
- 2 tsp butter
- ¼ cup chopped tomatoes
- Salt and black pepper to taste
- 1 cup pork rinds, crushed
- 1 tbsp chopped basil leaves
- 2 tbsp melted butter

Directions:

1. Preheat the oven to 350ºF and trim off the top and bottom ends of the zucchinis. Lay them flat on a chopping board, and cut a ¼ -inch off the top to create a boat for the stuffing. Scoop out the seeds with a spoon and set the zucchinis aside.
2. Melt the firm butter in a small skillet and sauté the onion and tomato for 6 minutes. Transfer the mixture to a bowl and add the shrimp, half of the pork rinds, basil leaves, salt, and pepper.
3. Combine the ingredients and stuff the zucchini boats with the mixture. Sprinkle the top of the boats with the remaining pork rinds and drizzle the melted butter over them.
4. Place them on a baking sheet and bake them for 15 to 20 minutes. The shrimp should no longer be pink by this time. Remove the zucchinis after and serve with a tomato and mozzarella salad.

Nutrition Info:

- Per Servings 3.2g Carbs, 24.6g Protein, 14.4g Fat, 135 Calories

Avocado And Salmon

Serves: 2 | Cooking Time: 0 Minutes

Ingredients:

- 1 avocado, halved, pitted
- 2 oz flaked salmon, packed in water
- 1 tbsp mayonnaise
- 1 tbsp grated cheddar cheese
- Seasoning:
- 1/8 tsp salt
- 2 tbsp coconut oil

Directions:

1. Prepare the avocado and for this, cut avocado in half and then remove its seed.Drain the salmon, add it in a bowl along with remaining ingredients, stir well and then scoop into the hollow on an avocado half.Serve.

Nutrition Info:

- 3 g Carbs; 19 g Protein; 48 g Fats; 525 Calories

Baked Codfish With Lemon

Serves: 4 | Cooking Time:25 Minutes

Ingredients:
- 4 fillets codfish
- 1 teaspoon salt
- 1 teaspoon pepper
- 2 tablespoons olive oil
- 2 teaspoons dried basil
- 2 tablespoons melted butter
- 1 teaspoon dried thyme
- 1/3 teaspoon onion powder
- 2 lemons, juiced
- lemon wedges, for garnish

Directions:

1. Preheat the oven to 400°F.
2. In a medium bowl combine the lemon juice, onion powder, olive oil, dried basil and thyme. Stir well. Season the fillets with salt and pepper.
3. Top each fillet into the mixture. Then place the fillets into a medium baking dish, greased with melted butter.
4. Bake the codfish fillets for 15-20 minutes. Serve with fresh lemon wedges. Enjoy!

Nutrition Info:
- Per serving: 3.9g Carbs; 21.2g Protein; 23.6g Fat; 308 Calories

Angel Hair Shirataki With Creamy Shrimp

Serves:4 | Cooking Time: 25 Minutes

Ingredients:
- 2 (8 oz) packs angel hair shirataki noodles
- 1 tbsp olive oil
- 1 lb shrimp, deveined
- 2 tbsp unsalted butter
- 6 garlic cloves, minced
- ½ cup dry white wine
- 1 ½ cups heavy cream
- ½ cup grated Asiago cheese
- 2 tbsp chopped fresh parsley

Directions:

1. Heat olive oil in a skillet, season the shrimp with salt and pepper, and cook on both sides, 2 minutes; set aside. Melt butter in the skillet and sauté garlic. Stir in wine and cook until reduced by half, scraping the bottom of the pan to deglaze. Stir in heavy cream. Let simmer for 1 minute and stir in Asiago cheese to melt. Return the shrimp to the sauce and sprinkle the parsley on top. Bring 2 cups of water to a boi. Strain shirataki pasta and rinse under hot running water. Allow proper draining and pour the shirataki pasta into the boiling water. Cook for 3 minutes and strain again. Place a dry skillet and stir-fry the pasta until dry, 1-2 minutes. Season with salt and plate. Top with the shrimp sauce and serve.

Nutrition Info:
- Per Serves 6.3g Carbs; 33g Protein ; 32g Fats; 493 Calories

Lemon Garlic Shrimp

Servings: 6 | Cooking Time: 22 Minutes

Ingredients:

- ½ cup butter, divided
- 2 lb shrimp, peeled and deveined
- Pink salt and black pepper to taste
- ¼ tsp sweet paprika
- 1 tbsp minced garlic
- 3 tbsp water
- 1 lemon, zested and juiced
- 2 tbsp chopped parsley

Directions:

1. Melt half of the butter in a large skillet over medium heat, season the shrimp with salt, pepper, paprika, and add to the butter. Stir in the garlic and cook the shrimp for 4 minutes on both sides until pink. Remove to a bowl and set aside.
2. Put the remaining butter in the skillet; include the lemon zest, juice, and water. Cook until the butter has melted, about 1 minute. Add the shrimp, parsley, and adjust the taste with salt and black pepper. Cook for 2 minutes on low heat. Serve the shrimp and sauce with squash pasta.

Nutrition Info:

- Per Servings 2g Carbs, 13g Protein, 22g Fat, 258 Calories

Bacon Wrapped Mahi-mahi

Serves: 2 | Cooking Time: 12 Minutes

Ingredients:

- 2 fillets of mahi-mahi
- 2 strips of bacon
- ½ of lime, zested
- 4 basil leaves
- ½ tsp salt
- Seasoning:
- ½ tsp ground black pepper
- 1 tbsp avocado oil

Directions:

1. Turn on the oven, then set it to 375 °F and let them preheat. Meanwhile, season fillets with salt and black pepper, top each fillet with 2 basil leaves, sprinkle with lime zest, wrap with a bacon strip and secure with a toothpick if needed. Take a medium skillet pan, place it over medium-high heat, add oil and when hot, place prepared fillets in it and cook for 2 minutes per side. Transfer pan into the oven and bake the fish for 5 to 7 minutes until thoroughly cooked. Serve.

Nutrition Info:

- 1.2 g Carbs; 27.1 g Protein; 11.3 g Fats; 217 Calories

Bang Bang Shrimps

Serves: 2 | Cooking Time: 6 Minutes

Ingredients:

- 4 oz shrimps¼ tsp paprika
- ¼ tsp apple cider vinegar
- 2 tbsp sweet chili sauce
- ¼ cup mayonnaise
- Seasoning:
- ¼ tsp salt
- 1/8 tsp ground black pepper
- 2 tsp avocado oil

Directions:

1. Take a medium skillet pan, place it over medium heat, add oil and wait until it gets hot.Season shrimps with salt, black pepper, and paprika until coated, add them to the pan, and cook for 2 to 3 minutes per side until pink and cooked.Take a medium bowl, place mayonnaise in it, and then whisk in vinegar and chili sauce until combined.Add shrimps into the mayonnaise mixture, toss until coated, and then serve.

Nutrition Info:

- 7.2 g Carbs; 13 g Protein; 23.1 g Fats; 290 Calories

Flounder With Dill And Capers

Servings: 4 | Cooking Time: 15 Minutes

Ingredients:

- 4 flounder fillets
- 1 tbsp. chopped fresh dill
- 2 tbsp. capers, chopped
- 4 lemon wedges
- 6 tbsp olive oil
- Salt and pepper to taste

Directions:

1. Place a trivet in a large saucepan and pour a cup or two of water into the pan. Bring to a boil.
2. Place flounder in a heatproof dish that fits inside a saucepan. Season snapper with pepper and salt. Drizzle with olive oil on all sides. Sprinkle dill and capers on top of the filet.
3. Seal dish with foil. Place the dish on the trivet inside the saucepan. Cover and steam for 15 minutes.
4. Serve and enjoy with lemon wedges.

Nutrition Info:

- Per Servings 8.6g Carbs, 20.3g Protein, 35.9g Fat, 447 Calories

Vegan, Vegetable & Meatless Recipes

Vegan, Vegetable & Meatless Recipes

Mushroom & Cauliflower Bake

Servings: 4 | Cooking Time: 30 Minutes

Ingredients:

- Cooking spray
- 1 head cauliflower, cut into florets
- 8 ounces mushrooms, halved
- 2 garlic cloves, smashed
- 2 tomatoes, pureed
- ¼ cup coconut oil, melted
- 1 tsp chili paprika paste
- ¼ tsp marjoram
- ½ tsp curry powder
- Salt and black pepper, to taste

Directions:

1. Set oven to 390°F. Apply a cooking spray to a baking dish. Lay mushrooms and cauliflower in the baking dish. Around the vegetables, scatter smashed garlic. Place in the pureed tomatoes. Sprinkle over melted coconut oil and place in chili paprika paste, curry, black pepper, salt, and marjoram. Roast for 25 minutes, turning once. Place in a serving plate and serve with green salad.

Nutrition Info:

- Per Servings 11.6g Carbs, 5g Protein, 6.7g Fat, 113 Calories

Bell Pepper Stuffed Avocado

Servings: 8 | Cooking Time: 10 Minutes

Ingredients:

- 4 avocados, pitted and halved
- 2 tbsp olive oil
- 3 cups green bell peppers, chopped
- 1 onion, chopped
- 1 tsp garlic puree
- Salt and black pepper, to taste
- 1 tsp deli mustard
- 1 tomato, chopped

Directions:

1. From each half of the avocados, scoop out 2 teaspoons of flesh; set aside.
2. Use a sauté pan to warm oil over medium-high heat. Cook the garlic, onion, and bell peppers until tender. Mix in the reserved avocado. Add in tomato, salt, mustard, and black pepper. Separate the mushroom mixture and mix equally among the avocado halves and serve.

Nutrition Info:

- Per Servings 7.4g Carbs, 2.4g Protein, 23.2g Fat, 255 Calories

Tofu Sandwich With Cabbage Slaw

Servings: 4 | Cooking Time: 4 Hours 10 Minutes

Ingredients:

- ½ lb Firm tofu, sliced
- 4 low carb buns
- 1 tbsp olive oil
- Marinade
- Salt and black pepper to taste
- 2 tsp allspice
- 1 tbsp erythritol
- 2 tsp chopped thyme
- 1 Habanero, seeded and minced
- 3 green onions, thinly sliced
- 2 cloves garlic
- ¼ cup olive oil
- Slaw
- ½ small cabbage, shredded
- 1 carrot, grated
- ½ red onion, grated
- 2 tsp swerve
- 2 tbsp white vinegar
- 1 pinch Italian seasoning
- ¼ cup olive oil
- 1 tsp Dijon mustard
- Salt and black pepper to taste

Directions:

1. In a food processor, make the marinade by blending the allspice, salt, black pepper, erythritol, thyme, habanero, green onions, garlic, and olive oil, for a minute. Pour the mixture in a bowl and put the tofu in it, coating it to be covered with marinade. Place in the fridge to marinate for 4 hours.
2. Make the slaw next: In a large bowl, evenly combine the white vinegar, swerve, olive oil, Dijon mustard, Italian seasoning, salt, and pepper. Stir in the cabbage, carrot, and onion, and place it in the refrigerator to chill while the tofu marinates.
3. Frying the tofu: heat 1 teaspoon of oil in a skillet over medium heat, remove the tofu from the marinade, and cook it in the oil to brown on both sides for 6 minutes in total. Remove onto a plate after and toast the buns in the skillet. In the buns, add the tofu and top with the slaw. Close the bread and serve with a sweet chili sauce.

Nutrition Info:

- Per Servings 7.8g Carbs, 14g Protein, 33g Fat, 386 Calories

Morning Granola

Servings: 8 | Cooking Time: 1 Hour

Ingredients:

- 1 tbsp coconut oil
- ⅓ cup almond flakes
- ½ cups almond milk
- 2 tbsp sugar
- 1/8 tsp salt
- 1 tsp lime zest
- 1/8 tsp nutmeg, grated
- ½ tsp ground cinnamon
- ½ cup pecans, chopped
- ½ cup almonds, slivered
- 2 tbsp pepitas
- 3 tbsp sunflower seeds
- ¼ cup flax seed

Directions:

1. Set a deep pan over medium-high heat and warm the coconut oil. Add almond flakes and toast for 1 to 2 minutes. Stir in the remaining ingredients. Set oven to 300ºF. Lay the mixture in an even layer onto a baking sheet lined with a parchment paper. Bake for 1 hour, making sure that you shake gently in intervals of 15 minutes. Serve alongside additional almond milk.

Nutrition Info:

- Per Servings 9.2g Carbs, 5.1g Protein, 24.3g Fat, 262 Calories

Sausage Roll

Servings: 6 | Cooking Time: 1 Hour And 15 Minutes

Ingredients:

- 6 vegan sausages (defrosted)
- 1 cup mushrooms
- 1 onion
- 2 fresh sage leaves
- 1 package tofu skin sheet
- Salt and pepper to taste
- 5 tablespoons olive oil

Directions:

1. Preheat the oven to 180°F/356°F assisted.
2. Defrost the vegan sausages.
3. Roughly chop the mushrooms and add them to a food processor. Process until mostly broken down. Peel and roughly chop the onions, then add them to the processor along with the defrosted vegan sausages, sage leaves, and a pinch of salt and pepper. Pour in the oil. Process until all the ingredients have mostly broken down, and only a few larger pieces remain.
4. Heat a frying pan on a medium heat. Once hot, transfer the mushroom mixture to the pan and fry for 20 minutes or until almost all of the moisture has evaporated, frequently stirring to prevent the mixture sticking to the pan.
5. Remove the mushroom mixture from the heat and transfer to a plate. Leave to cool completely. Tip: if it's cold outside, we leave the mushroom mixture outdoors, so it cools quicker.
6. Meanwhile, either line a large baking tray with baking paper or (if the pastry already comes wrapped in a sheet of baking paper) roll out the tofu skin onto the tray and cut it in half both lengthways and widthways to create 4 equal-sized pieces of tofu skin.
7. Spoon a quarter of the mushroom mixture along the length of each rectangle of tofu skin and shape the mixture into a log. Add one vegan sausage and roll into a log.
8. Seal the roll by securing the edged with a toothpick.
9. Brush the sausage rolls with olive oil and bake for 40-45 minutes until golden brown. Enjoy!

Nutrition Info:

- Per Servings 3g Carbs, 0.9g Protein, 11g Fat, 113 Calories

Zucchini Noodles

Servings: 6 | Cooking Time: 15 Mins

Ingredients:

- 2 cloves garlic, minced
- 2 medium zucchini, cut into noodles with a spiralizer
- 12 zucchini blossoms, pistils removed; cut into strips
- 6 fresh basil leaves, cut into strips, or to taste
- 4 tablespoons olive oil
- Salt to taste

Directions:

1. In a large skillet over low heat, cook garlic in olive oil for 10 minutes until slightly browned. Add in zucchini and zucchini blossoms, stir well.
2. Toss in green beans and season with salt to taste; sprinkle with basil and serve.

Nutrition Info:

- Per Servings 13.5g Carbs, 5.7g Protein, 28.1g Fat, 348 Calories

Pumpkin Bake

Servings: 6 | Cooking Time: 45 Minutes

Ingredients:

- 3 large Pumpkins, peeled and sliced
- 1 cup almond flour
- 1 cup grated mozzarella cheese
- 2 tbsp olive oil
- ½ cup chopped parsley

Directions:

1. Preheat the oven to 350ºF. Arrange the pumpkin slices in a baking dish, drizzle with olive oil, and bake for 35 minutes. Mix the almond flour, cheese, and parsley and when the pumpkin is ready, remove it from the oven, and sprinkle the cheese mixture all over. Place back in the oven and grill the top for 5 minutes.

Nutrition Info:

- Per Servings 5.7g Carbs, 2.7g Protein, 4.8g Fat, 125 Calories

Greek Styled Veggie-rice

Servings: 3 | Cooking Time: 20 Minutes

Ingredients:

- 3 tbsp chopped fresh mint
- 1 small tomato, chopped
- 1 head cauliflower, cut into large florets
- ¼ cup fresh lemon juice
- ½ yellow onion, minced
- pepper and salt to taste
- ¼ cup extra virgin olive oil

Directions:

1. In a bowl, mix lemon juice and onion and leave for 30 minutes. Then drain onion and reserve the juice and onion bits.
2. In a blender, shred cauliflower until the size of a grain of rice.
3. On medium fire, place a medium nonstick skillet and for 8-10 minutes cook cauliflower while covered.
4. Add grape tomatoes and cook for 3 minutes while stirring occasionally.
5. Add mint and onion bits. Cook for another three minutes.
6. Meanwhile, in a small bowl whisk pepper, salt, 3 tbsp reserved lemon juice, and olive oil until well blended.
7. Remove cooked cauliflower, transfer to a serving bowl, pour lemon juice mixture, and toss to mix.
8. Before serving, if needed season with pepper and salt to taste.

Nutrition Info:

- Per Servings 4.0g Carbs, 2.3g Protein, 9.5g Fat, 120 Calories

Herbed Portobello Mushrooms

Servings: 2 | Cooking Time: 10 Minutes

Ingredients:

- 2 Portobello mushrooms, stemmed and wiped clean
- 1 tsp minced garlic
- ¼ tsp dried rosemary
- 1 tablespoon balsamic vinegar
- ¼ cup grated provolone cheese
- 4 tablespoons olive oil
- Salt and pepper to taste

Directions:

1. In an oven, position rack 4-inches away from the top and preheat broiler.
2. Prepare a baking dish by spraying with cooking spray lightly.
3. Stemless, place mushroom gill side up.
4. Mix well garlic, rosemary, balsamic vinegar, and olive oil in a small bowl. Season with salt and pepper to taste.
5. Drizzle over mushrooms equally.
6. Marinate for at least 5 minutes before popping into the oven and broiling for 4 minutes per side or until tender.
7. Once cooked, remove from oven, sprinkle cheese, return to broiler and broil for a minute or two or until cheese melts.
8. Remove from oven and serve right away.

Nutrition Info:

- Per Servings 21.5g Carbs, 8.6g Protein, 5.1g Fat, 168 Calories

Mushroom & Jalapeño Stew

Servings: 4 | Cooking Time: 50 Minutes

Ingredients:

- 2 tsp olive oil
- 1 cup leeks, chopped
- 1 garlic clove, minced
- ½ cup celery, chopped
- ½ cup carrot, chopped
- 1 green bell pepper, chopped
- 1 jalapeño pepper, chopped
- 2 ½ cups mushrooms, sliced
- 1 ½ cups vegetable stock
- 2 tomatoes, chopped
- 2 thyme sprigs, chopped
- 1 rosemary sprig, chopped
- 2 bay leaves
- ½ tsp salt
- ¼ tsp ground black pepper
- 2 tbsp vinegar

Directions:

1. Set a pot over medium-high heat and warm oil. Add in garlic and leeks and sauté until soft and translucent. Add in the pepper, celery, mushrooms, and carrots.
2. Cook as you stir for 12 minutes; stir in a splash of vegetable stock to ensure there is no sticking. Stir in the rest of the ingredients. Set heat to medium; allow to simmer for 25 to 35 minutes or until cooked through. Divide into individual bowls and serve while warm.

Nutrition Info:

- Per Servings 9g Carbs, 2.7g Protein, 2.7g Fat, 65 Calories

Egg And Tomato Salad

Servings: 2 | Cooking Time: 1 Minute

Ingredients:

- 4 hard-boiled eggs, peeled and sliced
- 2 red tomatoes, chopped
- 1 small red onion, chopped
- 2 tablespoons lemon juice, freshly squeezed
- Salt and pepper to taste
- 4 tablespoons olive oil

Directions:

1. Place all ingredients in a mixing bowl.
2. Toss to coat all ingredients.
3. Garnish with parsley if desired.
4. Serve over toasted whole wheat bread.

Nutrition Info:

- Per Servings 9.1g Carbs, 14.7g Protein, 15.9g Fat, 189 Calories

Garlic And Greens

Servings: 4 | Cooking Time: 20 Minutes

Ingredients:

- 1-pound kale, trimmed and torn
- 1/4 cup chopped oil-packed sun-dried tomatoes
- 5 garlic cloves, minced
- 2 tablespoons minced fresh parsley
- 1/4 teaspoon salt
- 3 tablespoons olive oil

Directions:

1. In a 6-qt. stockpot, bring 1 inch. of water to a boil. Add kale; cook, covered, 10-15 minutes or until tender. Remove with a slotted spoon; discard cooking liquid.
2. In the same pot, heat oil over medium heat. Add tomatoes and garlic; cook and stir 1 minute. Add kale, parsley and salt; heat through, stirring occasionally.

Nutrition Info:

- Per Servings 9g Carbs, 6g Protein, 13g Fat, 160 Calories

Bianca Pizza

Servings: 1 | Cooking Time: 17 Minutes

Ingredients:

- 2 large eggs
- 1 tbsp water
- ½ jalapeño, diced
- 1 ounce Monterey Jack cheese, shredded
- 1 tbsp chopped green onions
- 1 cup egg Alfredo sauce
- ¼ tsp cumin
- 2 tbsp olive oil

Directions:

1. Preheat the oven to 350ºF.
2. Heat the olive oil in a skillet. Whisk the eggs along with water and cumin. Pour the eggs into the skillet. Cook until set. Top with the alfredo sauce and jalapeno. Sprinkle the green onions and cheese over. Place in the oven and bake for 5 minutes.

Nutrition Info:

- Per Servings 2g Carbs, 22g Protein, 55g Fat, 591 Calories

Parmesan Roasted Cabbage

Servings: 4 | Cooking Time: 25 Minutes

Ingredients:

- Cooking spray
- 1 large head green cabbage
- 4 tbsp melted butter
- 1 tsp garlic powder
- Salt and black pepper to taste
- 1 cup grated Parmesan cheese
- Grated Parmesan cheese for topping
- 1 tbsp chopped parsley to garnish

Directions:

1. Preheat oven to 400°F, line a baking sheet with foil, and grease with cooking spray.
2. Stand the cabbage and run a knife from the top to bottom to cut the cabbage into wedges. Remove stems and wilted leaves. Mix the butter, garlic, salt, and black pepper until evenly combined.
3. Brush the mixture on all sides of the cabbage wedges and sprinkle with parmesan cheese.
4. Place on the baking sheet, and bake for 20 minutes to soften the cabbage and melt the cheese. Remove the cabbages when golden brown, plate and sprinkle with extra cheese and parsley. Serve warm with pan-glazed tofu.

Nutrition Info:

- Per Servings 4g Carbs, 17.5g Protein, 19.3g Fat, 268 Calories

Lemon Grilled Veggie

Servings: 4 | Cooking Time: 20 Minutes

Ingredients:

- 2/3 eggplant
- 1 zucchini
- 10 oz. cheddar cheese
- 20 black olives
- 2 oz. leafy greens
- ½ cup olive oil
- 1 lemon, the juice
- 1 cup mayonnaise
- 4 tbsp almonds
- Salt and pepper

Directions:

1. Cut eggplant and zucchini lengthwise into half inch-thick slices. Season with salt to coat evenly. Set aside for 5-10 minutes.
2. Preheat the oven to 450 degrees F.
3. Pat zucchini and eggplant slices' surface dry with a kitchen towel.
4. Line a baking sheet with parchment paper and place slices on it. Spray with olive oil on top and season with pepper.
5. Bake for 15-20 minutes or until cooked through, flipping halfway.
6. Once done, transfer to a serving platter. Drizzle olive oil and lemon juice on top.
7. Serve with cheese cubes, almonds, olives, mayonnaise and leafy greens.

Nutrition Info:

- Per Servings 9g Carbs, 21g Protein, 99g Fat, 1013 Calories

Grilled Spicy Eggplant

Servings: 2 | Cooking Time: 20 Minutes

Ingredients:

- 2 small eggplants, cut into 1/2-inch slices
- 1/4 cup olive oil
- 2 tablespoons lime juice
- 3 teaspoons Cajun seasoning
- Salt and pepper to taste

Directions:

1. Brush eggplant slices with oil. Drizzle with lime juice; sprinkle with Cajun seasoning. Let stand for 5 minutes.
2. Grill eggplant, covered, over medium heat or broil 4 minutes. from heat until tender, 4-5 minutes per side.
3. Season with pepper and salt to taste.
4. Serve and enjoy.

Nutrition Info:

- Per Servings 7g Carbs, 5g Protein, 28g Fat, 350 Calories

Spicy Cauliflower Steaks With Steamed Green Beans

Servings: 4 | Cooking Time: 20 Minutes

Ingredients:

- 2 heads cauliflower, sliced lengthwise into 'steaks'
- ¼ cup olive oil
- ¼ cup chili sauce
- 2 tsp erythritol
- Salt and black pepper to taste
- 2 shallots, diced
- 1 bunch green beans, trimmed
- 2 tbsp fresh lemon juice
- 1 cup water
- Dried parsley to garnish

Directions:

1. In a bowl, mix the olive oil, chili sauce, and erythritol. Brush the cauliflower with the mixture. Place them on the grill, close the lid, and grill for 6 minutes. Flip the cauliflower, cook further for 6 minutes.
2. Bring the water to boil over high heat, place the green beans in a sieve and set over the steam from the boiling water. Cover with a clean napkin to keep the steam trapped in the sieve. Cook for 6 minutes. After, remove to a bowl and toss with lemon juice.
3. Remove the grilled caulis to a plate; sprinkle with salt, pepper, shallots, and parsley. Serve with the steamed green beans.

Nutrition Info:

- Per Servings 4g Carbs, 2g Protein, 9g Fat, 118 Calories

Briam With Tomato Sauce

Servings: 4 | Cooking Time: 70 Minutes

Ingredients:

- 3 tbsp olive oil
- 1 large eggplant, halved and sliced
- 1 large onion, thinly sliced
- 3 cloves garlic, sliced
- 5 tomatoes, diced
- 3 rutabagas, peeled and diced
- 1 cup sugar-free tomato sauce
- 4 zucchinis, sliced
- ¼ cup water
- Salt and black pepper to taste
- 1 tbsp dried oregano
- 2 tbsp chopped parsley

Directions:

1. Preheat the oven to 400ºF. Heat the olive oil in a skillet over medium heat and cook the eggplants in it for 6 minutes to brown on the edges. After, remove to a medium bowl.
2. Sauté the onion and garlic in the oil for 3 minutes and add them to the eggplants. Turn the heat off.
3. In the eggplants bowl, mix in the tomatoes, rutabagas, tomato sauce, and zucchinis. Add the water and stir in the salt, pepper, oregano, and parsley. Pour the mixture in the casserole dish. Place the dish in the oven and bake for 45 to 60 minutes. Serve the briam warm on a bed of cauli rice.

Nutrition Info:

- Per Servings 12.5g Carbs, 11.3g Protein, 12g Fat, 365 Calories

Vegetarian Burgers

Servings: 2 | Cooking Time: 20 Minutes

Ingredients:

- 1 garlic cloves, minced
- 2 portobello mushrooms, sliced
- 1 tbsp coconut oil, melted
- 1 tbsp chopped basil
- 1 tbsp oregano
- 2 eggs, fried
- 2 low carb buns
- 2 tbsp mayonnaise
- 2 lettuce leaves

Directions:

1. Combine the melted coconut oil, garlic, herbs, and salt, in a bowl. Place the mushrooms in the bowl and coat well. Preheat the grill to medium heat. Grill the mushrooms for 2 minutes per side.
2. Cut the low carb buns in half. Add the lettuce leaves, grilled mushrooms, eggs, and mayonnaise. Top with the other bun half.

Nutrition Info:

- Per Servings 8.5g Carbs, 23g Protein, 55g Fat, 637 Calories

Grilled Cauliflower

Servings: 8 | Cooking Time: 20 Minutes

Ingredients:

- 1 large head cauliflower
- 1 teaspoon ground turmeric
- 1/2 teaspoon crushed red pepper flakes
- Lemon juice, additional olive oil, and pomegranate seeds, optional
- 2 tablespoons olive oil
- 2 tablespoons melted butter

Directions:

1. Remove leaves and trim stem from cauliflower. Cut cauliflower into eight wedges. Mix turmeric and pepper flakes. Brush wedges with oil; sprinkle with turmeric mixture.
2. Grill, covered, over medium-high heat or broil 4 minutes from heat until cauliflower is tender, 8-10 minutes on each side. If desired, drizzle with lemon juice and additional oil. Brush with melted butter and serve with pomegranate seeds.

Nutrition Info:

- Per Servings 2.3g Carbs, 0.7g Protein, 6.3g Fat, 66 Calories

Cauliflower & Hazelnut Salad

Servings: 4 | Cooking Time: 15 Minutes + Chilling Time

Ingredients:

- 1 head cauliflower, cut into florets
- 1 cup green onions, chopped
- 4 ounces bottled roasted peppers, chopped
- ¼ cup extra-virgin olive oil
- 1 tbsp wine vinegar
- 1 tsp yellow mustard
- Salt and black pepper, to taste
- ½ cup black olives, pitted and chopped
- ½ cup hazelnuts, chopped

Directions:

1. Place the cauliflower florets over low heat and steam for 5 minutes; let cool and set aside. Add roasted peppers and green onions in a salad bowl.
2. Using a mixing dish, combine salt, olive oil, mustard, pepper, and vinegar. Sprinkle the mixture over the veggies. Place in the reserved cauliflower and shake to mix well. Top with hazelnut and black olives and serve.

Nutrition Info:

- Per Servings 6.6g Carbs, 4.2g Protein, 18g Fat, 221 Calories

Vegetable Greek Mousaka

Servings: 6 | Cooking Time: 50 Minutes

Ingredients:

- 2 large eggplants, cut into strips
- 1 cup diced celery
- 1 cup diced carrots
- 1 small white onion, chopped
- 2 eggs
- 1 tsp olive oil
- 3 cups grated Parmesan, divided into 2
- 1 cup ricotta cheese
- 3 cloves garlic, minced
- 2 tsp Italian seasoning blend
- Salt to taste
- Sauce:
- 1 ½ cups heavy cream
- ¼ cup butter, melted
- 1 cup grated mozzarella cheese
- 2 tsp Italian seasoning
- ¾ cup almond flour

Directions:

1. Preheat the oven to 350°F. Lay the eggplant strips on a paper towel, sprinkle with salt and let sit there to exude liquid. Heat olive oil in a skillet over medium heat and sauté the onion, celery, and carrots for 5 minutes. Stir in the garlic and cook further for 30 seconds; set aside to cool.

2. Mix the eggs, 1 cup of parmesan cheese, ricotta cheese, and salt in a bowl; set aside. Pour the heavy cream in a pot and bring to heat over a medium fire while continually stirring. Stir in the remaining parmesan cheese, and 1 teaspoon of Italian seasoning. Turn the heat off and set aside.

3. To lay the mousaka, spread a small amount of the sauce at the bottom of the baking dish. Pat dry the eggplant strips and make a single layer on the sauce. Spread a layer of ricotta cheese on the eggplants, sprinkle some veggies on it, and repeat the layering process from the sauce until all the ingredients are exhausted.

4. In a small bowl, evenly mix the melted butter, almond flour, and 1 teaspoon of Italian seasoning. Spread the top of the mousaka layers with it and sprinkle the top with mozzarella cheese. Cover the dish with foil and place it in the oven to bake for 25 minutes. Remove the foil and bake for 5 minutes until the cheese is slightly burned. Slice the mousaka and serve warm.

Nutrition Info:

- Per Servings 9.6g Carbs, 33g Protein, 35g Fat, 476 Calories

Morning Coconut Smoothie

Servings: 4 | Cooking Time: 5 Minutes

Ingredients:

- ½ cup water
- 1 ½ cups coconut milk
- 1 cup frozen cherries
- 4 cup fresh blueberries
- ¼ tsp vanilla extract
- 1 tbsp vegan protein powder

Directions:

1. Using a blender, combine all the ingredients and blend well until you attain a uniform and creamy consistency. Divide in glasses and serve!

Nutrition Info:

- Per Servings 14.9g Carbs, 2.6g Protein, 21.7g Fat, 247 Calories

Colorful Vegan Soup

Servings: 6 | Cooking Time: 25 Minutes

Ingredients:

- 2 tsp olive oil
- 1 red onion, chopped
- 2 cloves garlic, minced
- 1 celery stalk, chopped
- 1 head broccoli, chopped
- 1 carrot, sliced
- 1 cup spinach, torn into pieces
- 1 cup collard greens, chopped
- Sea salt and black pepper, to taste
- 2 thyme sprigs, chopped
- 1 rosemary sprig, chopped
- 2 bay leaves
- 6 cups vegetable stock
- 2 tomatoes, chopped
- 1 cup almond milk
- 1 tbsp white miso paste
- ½ cup arugula

Directions:

1. Place a large pot over medium-high heat and warm oil. Add in carrots, celery, onion, broccoli, garlic, and sauté until soft.
2. Place in spinach, salt, rosemary, tomatoes, bay leaves, ground black pepper, collard greens, thyme, and vegetable stock. On low heat, simmer the mixture for 15 minutes while the lid is slightly open.
3. Stir in white miso paste, watercress, and almond milk and cook for 5 more minutes.

Nutrition Info:

- Per Servings 9g Carbs, 2.9g Protein, 11.4g Fat, 142 Calories

Creamy Almond And Turnip Soup

Servings: 4 | Cooking Time: 25 Minutes

Ingredients:

- 1 tbsp olive oil
- 1 cup onion, chopped
- 1 celery, chopped
- 2 cloves garlic, minced
- 2 turnips, peeled and chopped
- 4 cups vegetable broth
- Salt and white pepper, to taste
- ¼ cup ground almonds
- 1 cup almond milk
- 1 tbsp fresh cilantro, chopped

Directions:

1. Set a stockpot over medium-high heat and warm the oil. Add in celery, garlic, and onion and sauté for 6 minutes. Stir in white pepper, broth, salt, and ground almonds. Boil the mixture. Set heat to low and simmer for 17 minutes. Transfer the soup to an immersion blender and puree. Decorate with fresh cilantro before serving.

Nutrition Info:

- Per Servings 9.2g Carbs, 3.8g Protein, 6.5g Fat, 114 Calories

Desserts And Drinks

Desserts And Drinks

Mint Chocolate Protein Shake

Servings: 4 | Cooking Time: 4 Minutes

Ingredients:

- 3 cups flax milk, chilled
- 3 tsp unsweetened cocoa powder
- 1 avocado, pitted, peeled, sliced
- 1 cup coconut milk, chilled
- 3 mint leaves + extra to garnish
- 3 tbsp erythritol
- 1 tbsp low carb Protein powder
- Whipping cream for topping

Directions:

1. Combine the milk, cocoa powder, avocado, coconut milk, mint leaves, erythritol, and protein powder into a blender, and blend for 1 minute until smooth.
2. Pour into serving glasses, lightly add some whipping cream on top, and garnish with mint leaves.

Nutrition Info:

- Per Servings 4g Carbs, 15g Protein, 14.5g Fat, 191 Calories

Coconut Bars

Servings: 4 | Cooking Time: 3 Hours

Ingredients:

- 3 ½ ounces ghee
- 10 saffron threads
- 1 ⅓ cups coconut milk
- 1 ¾ cups shredded coconut
- 4 tbsp sweetener
- 1 tsp cardamom powder

Directions:

1. Combine the shredded coconut with 1 cup of the coconut milk. In another bowl, mix together the remaining coconut milk with the sweetener and saffron. Let sit for 30 minutes.
2. Heat the ghee in a wok. Add the coconut mixture as well as the saffron threads, and cook for 5 minutes on low heat, mixing continuously. Stir in the cardamom and cook for another 5 minutes.
3. Spread the mixture onto a small container and freeze for 2 hours. Cut into bars and enjoy!

Nutrition Info:

- Per Servings 1.4g Carbs, 2g Protein, 22g Fat, 215 Calories

Lemony-avocado Cilantro Shake

Servings: 1 | Cooking Time: 0 Minutes

Ingredients:

- ½ cup half and half
- 1 packet Stevia, or more to taste
- ¼ avocado, meat scooped
- 1 tbsp chopped cilantro
- 3 tbsps coconut oil
- 1 ½ cups water

Directions:

1. Add all ingredients in a blender.
2. Blend until smooth and creamy.
3. Serve and enjoy.

Nutrition Info:

- Per Servings 8.4g Carbs, 4.4g Protein, 49g Fat, 501 Calories

Keto Nut Bark

Servings: 8 | Cooking Time: 40 Minutes

Ingredients:

- 1 pound chopped walnuts
- 1-1/2 teaspoons ground cinnamon
- ½ cup butter, melted
- 1 packet stevia powder
- ½ cup coconut oil

Directions:

1. Preheat oven to 350°F. Coat a 13x9-in. baking dish with cooking spray. Combine walnuts and cinnamon.
2. Mix all ingredients until well combined.
3. Press on a baking sheet and flatten with a rolling pin.
4. Allow to harden in the fridge before breaking into barks.

Nutrition Info:

- Per Servings 7.9g Carbs, 9g Protein, 68g Fat, 648 Calories

White Choco Fatty Fudge

Servings: 6 | Cooking Time: 10 Minutes

Ingredients:

- 1/4 cup coconut butter
- 1/4 cup cashew butter
- 2 tbsp cacao butter
- 1/4 teaspoon vanilla powder
- 10–12 drops liquid stevia, or to taste
- 2 tbsp coconut oil

Directions:

1. Over low heat, place a small saucepan and melt coconut oil, cacao butter, cashew butter, and coconut butter.
2. Remove from the heat and stir in the vanilla and stevia.
3. Pour into a silicone mold and place it in the freezer for 30 minutes.
4. Store in the fridge for a softer consistency.

Nutrition Info:

- Per Servings 1.7g Carbs, 0.2g Protein, 23.7g Fat, 221 Calories

Raspberry-choco Shake

Servings: 1 | Cooking Time: 0 Minutes

Ingredients:

- ¼ cup heavy cream, liquid
- 1 tbsp cocoa powder
- 1 packet Stevia, or more to taste
- ¼ cup raspberries
- 1 ½ cups water

Directions:

1. Add all ingredients in a blender.
2. Blend until smooth and creamy.
3. Serve and enjoy.

Nutrition Info:

- Per Servings 11.1g Carbs, 3.8g Protein, 45.0g Fat, 438 Calories

Walnut Cookies

Servings: 12 | Cooking Time: 25 Minutes

Ingredients:

- 1 egg
- 2 cups ground pecans
- ¼ cup sweetener
- ½ tsp baking soda
- 1 tbsp butter
- 20 walnuts halves

Directions:

1. Preheat the oven to 350°F. Mix the ingredients, except the walnuts, until combined. Make 20 balls out of the mixture and press them with your thumb onto a lined cookie sheet. Top each cookie with a walnut half. Bake for about 12 minutes.

Nutrition Info:

- Per Servings 0.6g Carbs, 1.6g Protein, 11g Fat, 101 Calories

Nutty Choco Milk Shake

Servings: 1 | Cooking Time: 0 Minutes

Ingredients:

- ¼ cup half and half
- 1 tbsp cocoa powder
- 1 packet Stevia, or more to taste
- 4 pecans
- 1 tbsp macadamia oil
- 1 ½ cups water
- 3 tbsp coconut oil

Directions:

1. Add all ingredients in a blender.
2. Blend until smooth and creamy.
3. Serve and enjoy.

Nutrition Info:

- Per Servings 9.4g Carbs, 4.8g Protein, 73g Fat, 689 Calories

Eggnog Keto Custard

Servings: 8 | Cooking Time: 10 Minutes

Ingredients:

- ¼ tsp nutmeg
- ¼ Truvia
- ½ cup heavy whipping cream
- 1 cup half and half
- 4 eggs

Directions:

1. Blend all ingredients together.
2. Pour evenly into 6 ramekins (microwave safe).
3. Microwave at 50% power for 4 minutes then stir thoroughly.
4. Microwave for another 3-4 minutes at 50% power then stir well again.
5. Serve either cool or hot.

Nutrition Info:

- Per Servings 1.0g Carbs, 3.0g Protein, 6.0g Fat, 70 Calories

Cinnamon And Turmeric Latte

Servings: 4 | Cooking Time: 7 Minutes

Ingredients:

- 3 cups almond milk
- ⅓ tsp cinnamon powder
- 1 cup brewed coffee
- ½ tsp turmeric powder
- 1 ½ tsp erythritol
- Cinnamon sticks to garnish

Directions:

1. In the blender, add the almond milk, cinnamon powder, coffee, turmeric, and erythritol. Blend the ingredients at medium speed for 45 seconds and pour the mixture into a saucepan.
2. Set the pan over low heat and heat through for 5 minutes; do not boil. Keep swirling the pan to prevent from boiling. Turn the heat off, and serve in latte cups, with a cinnamon stick in each one.

Nutrition Info:

- Per Servings 0.3g Carbs, 3.9g Protein, 12g Fat, 132 Calories

Vanilla Bean Frappuccino

Servings: 4 | Cooking Time: 6 Minutes

Ingredients:

- 3 cups unsweetened vanilla almond milk, chilled
- 2 tsp swerve
- 1 ½ cups heavy cream, cold
- 1 vanilla bean
- ¼ tsp xanthan gum
- Unsweetened chocolate shavings to garnish

Directions:

1. Combine the almond milk, swerve, heavy cream, vanilla bean, and xanthan gum in the blender, and process on high speed for 1 minute until smooth. Pour into tall shake glasses, sprinkle with chocolate shavings, and serve immediately.

Nutrition Info:

- Per Servings 6g Carbs, 15g Protein, 14g Fat, 193 Calories

Coconut Cheesecake

Servings: 12 | Cooking Time: 4 Hours And 50 Minutes

Ingredients:

- Crust
- 2 egg whites
- ¼ cup erythritol
- 3 cups desiccated coconut
- 1 tsp coconut oil
- ¼ cup melted butter
- Filling:
- 3 tbsp lemon juice
- 6 ounces raspberries
- 2 cups erythritol
- 1 cup whipped cream
- Zest of 1 lemon
- 24 ounces cream cheese

Directions:

1. Apply the coconut oil to the bottom and sides of a springform pan. Line with parchment paper. Preheat your oven to 350°F and mix all crust ingredients. Pour the crust into the pan.
2. Bake for about 25 minutes; then let cool.
3. Meanwhile, beat the cream cheese with an electric mixer until soft. Add the lemon juice, zest, and erythritol.
4. Fold the whipped cream into the cheese cream mixture. Fold in the raspberries gently. Spoon the filling into the baked and cooled crust. Place in the fridge for 4 hours.

Nutrition Info:

- Per Servings 3g Carbs, 5g Protein, 25g Fat, 256 Calories

Passion Fruit Cheesecake Slices

Servings: 8 | Cooking Time: 2 Hours 30 Minutes

Ingredients:

- 1 cup crushed almond biscuits
- ½ cup melted butter
- Filling:
- 1 ½ cups cream cheese
- ¾ cup swerve
- 1 ½ whipping cream
- 1 tsp vanilla bean paste
- 4-6 tbsp cold water
- 1 tbsp gelatin powder
- Passionfruit Jelly
- 1 cup passion fruit pulp
- ¼ cup swerve confectioner's sugar
- 1 tsp gelatin powder
- ¼ cup water, room temperature

Directions:

1. Mix the crushed biscuits and butter in a bowl, spoon into a spring-form pan, and use the back of the spoon to level at the bottom. Set aside in the fridge. Put the cream cheese, swerve, and vanilla paste into a bowl, and use the hand mixer to whisk until smooth; set aside.
2. In a bowl, add 2 tbsp of cold water and sprinkle 1 tbsp of gelatin powder. Let dissolve for 5 minutes. Pour the gelatin liquid along with the whipping cream in the cheese mixture and fold gently.
3. Remove the spring-form pan from the refrigerator and pour over the mixture. Return to the fridge.
4. Repeat the dissolving process for the remaining gelatin and once your out of ingredients, pour the confectioner's sugar, and ¼ cup of water into it. Mix and stir in the passion fruit pulp.
5. Remove the cake again and pour the jelly over it. Swirl the pan to make the jelly level up. Place the pan back into the fridge to cool for 2 hours. When completely set, remove and unlock the spring-pan. Lift the pan from the cake and slice the dessert.

Nutrition Info:

- Per Servings 6.1g Carbs, 4.4g Protein, 18g Fat, 287 Calories

Raspberry Nut Truffles

Servings: 4 | Cooking Time: 6 Minutes + Cooling Time

Ingredients:

- 2 cups raw cashews
- 2 tbsp flax seed
- 1 ½ cups sugar-free raspberry preserves
- 3 tbsp swerve
- 10 oz unsweetened chocolate chips
- 3 tbsp olive oil

Directions:

1. Line a baking sheet with parchment paper and set aside. Grind the cashews and flax seeds in a blender for 45 seconds until smoothly crushed; add the raspberry and 2 tbsp of swerve.
2. Process further for 1 minute until well combined. Form 1-inch balls of the mixture, place on the baking sheet, and freeze for 1 hour or until firmed up.
3. Melt the chocolate chips, oil, and 1tbsp of swerve in a microwave for 1 ½ minutes. Toss the truffles to coat in the chocolate mixture, put on the baking sheet, and freeze further for at least 2 hours.

Nutrition Info:

- Per Servings 3.5g Carbs, 12g Protein, 18.3g Fat, 251 Calories

Creamy Coconut Kiwi Drink

Servings: 4 | Cooking Time: 3 Minutes

Ingredients:

- 6 kiwis, pulp scooped
- 3 tbsp erythritol or to taste
- 3 cups unsweetened coconut milk
- 2 cups coconut cream
- 7 ice cubes
- Mint leaves to garnish

Directions:

1. In a blender, process the kiwis, erythritol, milk, cream, and ice cubes until smooth, about 3 minutes. Pour into four serving glasses, garnish with mint leaves, and serve.

Nutrition Info:

- Per Servings 1g Carbs, 16g Protein, 38g Fat, 425 Calories

Coconut Fat Bombs

Servings: 4 | Cooking Time: 22 Minutes +cooling Time

Ingredients:

- 2/3 cup coconut oil, melted
- 1 can coconut milk
- 18 drops stevia liquid
- 1 cup unsweetened coconut flakes

Directions:

1. Mix the coconut oil with the milk and stevia to combine. Stir in the coconut flakes until well distributed. Pour into silicone muffin molds and freeze for 1 hour to harden.

Nutrition Info:

- Per Servings 2g Carbs, 4g Protein, 19g Fat, 214 Calories

Mixed Berry Trifle

Servings: 4 | Cooking Time: 3 Minutes + Cooling Time

Ingredients:

- ½ cup walnuts, toasted
- 1 avocado, chopped
- 1 cup mascarpone cheese, softened
- 1 cup fresh blueberries
- 1 cup fresh raspberries
- 1 cup fresh blackberries

Directions:

1. In four dessert glasses, share half of the mascarpone, half of the berries (mixed), half of the walnuts, and half of the avocado, and repeat the layering process for a second time to finish the ingredients. Cover the glasses with plastic wrap and refrigerate for 45 minutes until quite firm.

Nutrition Info:

- Per Servings 8.3g Carbs, 9.8g Protein, 28.5g Fat, 321 Calories

White Chocolate Cheesecake Bites

Servings: 12 | Cooking Time: 4 Minutes + Cooling Time

Ingredients:
- 10 oz unsweetened white chocolate chips
- ½ half and half
- 20 oz cream cheese, softened
- ½ cup swerve
- 1 tsp vanilla extract

Directions:

1. In a saucepan, melt the chocolate with half and a half on low heat for 1 minute. Turn the heat off.
2. In a bowl, whisk the cream cheese, swerve, and vanilla extract with a hand mixer until smooth. Stir into the chocolate mixture. Spoon into silicone muffin tins and freeze for 4 hours until firm.

Nutrition Info:
- Per Servings 3.1g Carbs, 5g Protein, 22g Fat, 241 Calories

Coconut Raspberry Bars

Servings: 12 | Cooking Time: 20 Minutes

Ingredients:
- 1 cup coconut milk
- 3 cups desiccated coconut
- 1/3 cup erythritol powder
- 1 cup raspberries, pulsed
- ½ cup coconut oil or other oils

Directions:

1. Preheat oven to 380oF.
2. Combine all ingredients in a mixing bowl.
3. Pour into a greased baking dish.
4. Bake in the oven for 20 minutes.
5. Let it rest for 10 minutes.
6. Serve and enjoy.

Nutrition Info:
- Per Servings 8.2g Carbs, 1.5g Protein, 14.7g Fat, 170 Calories

Almond Milk Hot Chocolate

Servings: 4 | Cooking Time: 7 Minutes

Ingredients:
- 3 cups almond milk
- 4 tbsp unsweetened cocoa powder
- 2 tbsp swerve
- 3 tbsp almond butter
- Finely chopped almonds to garnish

Directions:

1. In a saucepan, add the almond milk, cocoa powder, and swerve. Stir the mixture until the sugar dissolves. Set the pan over low to heat through for 5 minutes, without boiling.
2. Swirl the mix occasionally. Turn the heat off and stir in the almond butter to be incorporated. Pour the hot chocolate into mugs and sprinkle with chopped almonds. Serve warm.

Nutrition Info:
- Per Servings 0.6g Carbs, 4.5g Protein, 21.5g Fat, 225 Calories

Eggless Strawberry Mousse

Servings: 6 | Cooking Time: 6 Minutes + Cooling Time

Ingredients:

- 2 cups chilled heavy cream
- 2 cups fresh strawberries, hulled
- 5 tbsp erythritol
- 2 tbsp lemon juice
- ¼ tsp strawberry extract
- 2 tbsp sugar-free strawberry preserves

Directions:

1. Beat the heavy cream, in a bowl, with a hand mixer at high speed until a stiff peak forms, for about 1 minute; refrigerate immediately. Puree the strawberries in a blender and pour into a saucepan.
2. Add erythritol and lemon juice, and cook on low heat for 3 minutes while stirring continuously. Stir in the strawberry extract evenly, turn off heat and allow cooling. Fold in the whipped cream until evenly incorporated, and spoon into six ramekins. Refrigerate for 4 hours to solidify.
3. Garnish with strawberry preserves and serve immediately.

Nutrition Info:

- Per Servings 5g Carbs, 5g Protein, 24g Fat, 290 Calories

Chocolate Marshmallows

Servings: 4 | Cooking Time: 30 Minutes

Ingredients:

- 2 tbsp unsweetened cocoa powder
- ½ tsp vanilla extract
- ½ cup swerve
- 1 tbsp xanthan gum mixed in 1 tbsp water
- A pinch Salt
- 6 tbsp Cool water
- 2 ½ tsp Gelatin powder
- Dusting:
- 1 tbsp unsweetened cocoa powder
- 1 tbsp swerve confectioner's sugar

Directions:

1. Line the loaf pan with parchment paper and grease with cooking spray; set aside. In a saucepan, mix the swerve, 2 tbsp of water, xanthan gum mixture, and salt. Place the pan over medium heat and bring to a boil. Insert the thermometer and let the ingredients simmer to 238 F, for 7 minutes.
2. In a small bowl, add 2 tbsp of water and sprinkle the gelatin on top. Let sit there without stirring to dissolve for 5 minutes. While the gelatin dissolves, pour the remaining water in a small bowl and heat in the microwave for 30 seconds. Stir in cocoa powder and mix it into the gelatin.
3. When the sugar solution has hit the right temperature, gradually pour it directly into the gelatin mixture while continuously whisking. Beat for 10 minutes to get a light and fluffy consistency.
4. Next, stir in the vanilla and pour the blend into the loaf pan. Let the marshmallows set for 3 hours and then use an oiled knife to cut it into cubes; place them on a plate. Mix the remaining cocoa powder and confectioner's sugar together. Sift it over the marshmallows.

Nutrition Info:

- Per Servings 5.1g Carbs, 0.5g Protein, 2.2g Fat, 55 Calories

Cardamom-cinnamon Spiced Coco-latte

Servings: 1 | Cooking Time: 0 Minutes

Ingredients:

- ½ cup coconut milk
- ¼ tsp cardamom powder
- 1 tbsp chocolate powder
- 1 ½ cups brewed coffee, chilled
- 1 tbsp coconut oil
- ¼ tsp cinnamon
- ¼ tsp nutmeg

Directions:

1. Add all ingredients in a blender.
2. Blend until smooth and creamy.
3. Serve and enjoy.

Nutrition Info:

- Per Servings 7.5g Carbs, 3.8g Protein, 38.7g Fat, 362 Calories

Nutty Greens Shake

Servings: 1 | Cooking Time: 0 Minutes

Ingredients:

- ½ cup half and half, liquid
- 1 packet Stevia, or more to taste
- 3 pecan nuts
- 3 macadamia nuts
- 1 cup spring mix salad greens
- 1 ½ cups water
- 3 tablespoons coconut oil

Directions:

1. Add all ingredients in a blender.
2. Blend until smooth and creamy.
3. Serve and enjoy.

Nutrition Info:

- Per Servings 10.5g Carbs, 7.0g Protein, 65.6g Fat, 628 Calories

Italian Greens And Yogurt Shake

Servings: 1 | Cooking Time: 0 Minutes

Ingredients:

- ½ cup half and half
- ½ cup Italian greens
- 1 packet Stevia, or more to taste
- 1 tbsp hemp seeds
- 3 tbsp coconut oil
- 1 cup water

Directions:

1. Add all ingredients in a blender.
2. Blend until smooth and creamy.
3. Serve and enjoy.

Nutrition Info:

- Per Servings 10.3g Carbs, 5.2g Protein, 46.9g Fat, 476 Calories

Soups, Stew & Salads

Strawberry Salad With Spinach, Cheese & Almonds

Servings: 2 | Cooking Time: 20 Minutes

Ingredients:

- 4 cups spinach
- 4 strawberries, sliced
- ½ cup flaked almonds
- 1 ½ cup grated hard goat cheese
- 4 tbsp raspberry vinaigrette
- Salt and black pepper, to taste

Directions:

1. Preheat your oven to 400ºF. Arrange the grated goat cheese in two circles on two pieces of parchment paper. Place in the oven and bake for 10 minutes.
2. Find two same bowls, place them upside down, and carefully put the parchment paper on top to give the cheese a bowl-like shape. Let cool that way for 15 minutes. Divide spinach among the bowls stir in salt, pepper and drizzle with vinaigrette. Top with almonds and strawberries.

Nutrition Info:

- Per Servings 5.3g Carbs, 33g Protein, 34.2g Fat, 445 Calories

Chicken Cabbage Soup

Servings: 6 | Cooking Time: 30 Minutes

Ingredients:

- 1 can Italian-style tomatoes
- 3 cups chicken broth
- 1 chicken breast
- ½ head of cabbage, shredded
- 1 packet Italian seasoning mix
- Salt and pepper to taste
- 1 cup water
- 1 tsp oil

Directions:

1. Place a heavy-bottomed pot on medium fire and heat for a minute. Add oil and swirl to coat the bottom and sides of the pot.
2. Pan fry chicken breast for 4 minutes per side. Transfer to a chopping board and cut into ½-inch cubes.
3. Add all ingredients to the pot and stir well.
4. Cover and bring to a boil, lower fire to a simmer, and cook for 20 minutes.
5. Adjust seasoning to taste, serve, and enjoy.

Nutrition Info:

- Per Servings 5.6g Carbs, 34.1g Protein, 9.3g Fat, 248 Calories

Asparagus Niçoise Salad

Servings: 4 | Cooking Time: 0 Minutes

Ingredients:

- 1-pound fresh asparagus, trimmed and blanched
- 2 ½ ounces white tuna in oil
- ½ cup pitted Greek olives, halved
- ½ cup zesty Italian salad dressing
- Salt and pepper to taste
- 3 tablespoons olive oil

Directions:

1. Place all ingredients in a bowl.
2. Toss to mix all ingredients.
3. Serve.

Nutrition Info:

- Per Servings 10g Carbs, 8g Protein, 20g Fat, 239 Calories

Arugula Prawn Salad With Mayo Dressing

Servings: 4 | Cooking Time: 15 Minutes

Ingredients:

- 4 cups baby arugula
- ½ cup garlic mayonnaise
- 3 tbsp olive oil
- 1 lb tiger prawns, peeled and deveined
- 1 tsp Dijon mustard
- Salt and chili pepper to season
- 2 tbsp lemon juice

Directions:

1. Add the mayonnaise, lemon juice and mustard in a small bowl. Mix until smooth and creamy. Heat 2 tbps of olive oil in a skillet over medium heat, add the prawns, season with salt, and chili pepper, and fry in the oil for 3 minutes on each side until prawns are pink. Set aside to a plate.
2. Place the arugula in a serving bowl and pour half of the dressing on the salad. Toss with 2 spoons until mixed, and add the remaining dressing. Divide salad into 4 plates and serve with prawns.

Nutrition Info:

- Per Servings 2g Carbs, 8g Protein, 20.3g Fat, 215 Calories

Rustic Beef Soup

Servings: 4 | Cooking Time: 20 Minutes

Ingredients:

- 3 cups beef broth
- 2 cups frozen mixed vegetables
- 1 teaspoon ground mustard
- Beef roast
- 1 teaspoon water
- Pinch of salt

Directions:

1. In a large saucepan, combine all the ingredients.
2. Bring to a boil.
3. Reduce heat; simmer, uncovered, for 15-20 minutes or until barley is tender.

Nutrition Info:

- Per Servings 8g Carbs, 51g Protein, 24g Fat, 450 Calories

Tuna Salad With Lettuce & Olives

Servings: 2 | Cooking Time: 5 Minutes

Ingredients:

- 1 cup canned tuna, drained
- 1 tsp onion flakes
- 3 tbsp mayonnaise
- 1 cup shredded romaine lettuce
- 1 tbsp lime juice
- Sea salt, to taste
- 6 black olives, pitted and sliced

Directions:

1. Combine the tuna, mayonnaise, lime juice, and salt in a small bowl; mix to combine well. In a salad platter, arrange the shredded lettuce and onion flakes. Spread the tuna mixture over; top with black olives to serve.

Nutrition Info:

- Per Servings 2g Carbs, 18.5g Protein, 20g Fat, 248 Calories

Green Salad

Servings: 4 | Cooking Time: 30 Minutes

Ingredients:

- 2 cups green beans, chopped
- 2 cups shredded spinach
- ½ cup parmesan cheese
- 3 cups basil leaves
- 3 cloves of garlic
- Salt to taste
- ¼ cup olive oil

Directions:

1. Heat a little olive oil in a skillet over medium heat and add the green beans and season with salt to taste. Sauté for 3 to 5 minutes.
2. Place the green beans in a bowl and add in the spinach.
3. In a food processor, combine half of the parmesan cheese, basil, and garlic. Add in the rest of the oil and season with salt and pepper to taste.
4. Pour into the green beans and toss to coat the ingredients.

Nutrition Info:

- Per Servings 6g Carbs, 5g Protein, 17g Fat, 196 Calories

Brussels Sprouts Salad With Pecorino Romano

Servings: 6 | Cooking Time: 35 Minutes

Ingredients:

- 2 lb Brussels sprouts, halved
- 3 tbsp olive oil
- Salt and black pepper to taste
- 2 ½ tbsp balsamic vinegar
- ¼ red cabbage, shredded
- 1 tbsp Dijon mustard
- 1 cup pecorino romano cheese, grated

Directions:

1. Preheat oven to 400ºF and line a baking sheet with foil. Toss the brussels sprouts with olive oil, a little salt, black pepper, and balsamic vinegar, in a bowl, and spread on the baking sheet in an even layer. Bake until tender on the inside and crispy on the outside, about 20 to 25 minutes.
2. Transfer to a salad bowl and add the red cabbage, Dijon mustard and half of the cheese. Mix until well combined. Sprinkle with the remaining cheese, share the salad onto serving plates, and serve with syrup-grilled salmon.

Nutrition Info:

- Per Servings 6g Carbs, 4g Protein, 18g Fat, 210 Calories

Chicken And Cauliflower Rice Soup

Servings: 8 | Cooking Time: 20 Mins

Ingredients:

- 2 cooked, boneless chicken breast halves, shredded
- 2 packages Steamed Cauliflower Rice
- 1/4 cup celery, chopped
- 1/2 cup onion, chopped
- 4 garlic cloves, minced
- Salt and ground black pepper to taste
- 2 teaspoons poultry seasoning
- 4 cups chicken broth
- ½ cup butter
- 2 cups heavy cream

Directions:

1. Heat butter in a large pot over medium heat, add onion, celery and garlic cloves to cook until tender. Meanwhile, place the riced cauliflower steam bags in the microwave following directions on the package.
2. Add the riced cauliflower, seasoning, salt and black pepper to butter mixture, saute them for 7 minutes on medium heat, stirring constantly to well combined.
3. Bring cooked chicken breast halves, broth and heavy cream to a broil. When it starts boiling, lower the heat, cover and simmer for 15 minutes.

Nutrition Info:

- Per Servings 6g Carbs, 27g Protein, 30g Fat, 415 Calories

Chicken Creamy Soup

Servings: 4 | Cooking Time: 15 Minutes

Ingredients:

- 2 cups cooked and shredded chicken
- 3 tbsp butter, melted
- 4 cups chicken broth
- 4 tbsp chopped cilantro
- ⅓ cup buffalo sauce
- ½ cup cream cheese
- Salt and black pepper, to taste

Directions:

1. Blend the butter, buffalo sauce, and cream cheese, in a food processor, until smooth. Transfer to a pot, add the chicken broth and heat until hot but do not bring to a boil. Stir in chicken, salt, black pepper and cook until heated through. When ready, remove to soup bowls and serve garnished with cilantro.

Nutrition Info:

- Per Servings 5g Carbs, 26.5g Protein, 29.5g Fat, 406 Calories

Mediterranean Salad

Servings: 4 | Cooking Time: 10 Minutes

Ingredients:

- 3 tomatoes, sliced
- 1 large avocado, sliced
- 8 kalamata olives
- ¼ lb buffalo mozzarella cheese, sliced
- 2 tbsp pesto sauce
- 2 tbsp olive oil

Directions:

1. Arrange the tomato slices on a serving platter and place the avocado slices in the middle. Arrange the olives around the avocado slices and drop pieces of mozzarella on the platter. Drizzle the pesto sauce all over, and drizzle olive oil as well.

Nutrition Info:

- Per Servings 4.3g Carbs, 9g Protein, 25g Fat, 290 Calories

Green Mackerel Salad

Servings: 2 | Cooking Time: 25 Minutes

Ingredients:

- 2 mackerel fillets
- 2 hard-boiled eggs, sliced
- 1 tbsp coconut oil
- 2 cups green beans
- 1 avocado, sliced
- 4 cups mixed salad greens
- 2 tbsp olive oil
- 2 tbsp lemon juice
- 1 tsp Dijon mustard
- Salt and black pepper, to taste

Directions:

1. Fill a saucepan with water and add the green beans and salt. Cook over medium heat for about 3 minutes. Drain and set aside.
2. Melt the coconut oil in a pan over medium heat. Add the mackerel fillets and cook for about 4 minutes per side, or until opaque and crispy. Divide the green beans between two salad bowls. Top with mackerel, egg, and avocado slices.
3. In a bowl, whisk together the lemon juice, olive oil, mustard, salt, and pepper, and drizzle over the salad.

Nutrition Info:

- Per Servings 7.6g Carbs, 27.3g Protein, 41.9g Fat, 525 Calories

Insalata Caprese

Servings: 8 | Cooking Time: 0 Minutes

Ingredients:

- 2 ½ pounds tomatoes, cut into 1-in pieces
- 8 ounces mozzarella cheese pearls
- ½ cup ripe olives, pitted
- ¼ cup fresh basil, sliced thinly
- Balsamic vinegar (optional)
- Salt and pepper to taste
- 3 tablespoons olive oil

Directions:

1. Place all ingredients in a bowl.
2. Season with salt and pepper to taste. Drizzle with balsamic vinegar if available.
3. Toss to coat.
4. Serve immediately.

Nutrition Info:

- Per Servings 7g Carbs, 6g Protein, 12g Fat, 160 Calories

Thyme & Wild Mushroom Soup

Servings: 4 | Cooking Time: 25 Minutes

Ingredients:

- ¼ cup butter
- ½ cup crème fraiche
- 12 oz wild mushrooms, chopped
- 2 tsp thyme leaves
- 2 garlic cloves, minced
- 4 cups chicken broth
- Salt and black pepper, to taste

Directions:

1. Melt the butter in a large pot over medium heat. Add garlic and cook for one minute until tender. Add mushrooms, salt and pepper, and cook for 10 minutes. Pour the broth over and bring to a boil.
2. Reduce the heat and simmer for 10 minutes. Puree the soup with a hand blender until smooth. Stir in crème Fraiche. Garnish with thyme leaves before serving.

Nutrition Info:

- Per Servings 5.8g Carbs, 6.1g Protein, 25g Fat, 281 Calories

Coconut Cauliflower Soup

Servings: 10 | Cooking Time: 26 Minutes

Ingredients:

- 1 medium onion, finely chopped
- 3 tablespoons yellow curry paste
- 2 medium heads cauliflower, broken into florets
- 1 carton vegetable broth
- 1 cup coconut milk
- 2 tablespoons olive oil

Directions:

1. In a large saucepan, heat oil over medium heat. Add onion; cook and stir until softened, 2-3 minutes.
2. Add curry paste; cook until fragrant, 1-2 minutes.
3. Add cauliflower and broth. Increase heat to high; bring to a boil. Reduce heat to medium-low; cook, covered, about 20 minutes.
4. Stir in coconut milk; cook an additional minute.
5. Remove from heat; cool slightly.
6. Puree in batches in a blender or food processor.
7. If desired, top with minced fresh cilantro.

Nutrition Info:

- Per Servings 10g Carbs, 3g Protein, 8g Fat, 111 Calories

Kale And Brussels Sprouts

Servings: 6 | Cooking Time: 0 Minutes

Ingredients:

- 1 small bunch kale, thinly sliced
- ½ pound fresh Brussels sprouts, thinly sliced
- ½ cup pistachios, chopped coarsely
- ½ cup honey mustard salad dressing
- ¼ cup parmesan cheese, shredded
- Salt and pepper to taste

Directions:

1. Place all ingredients in a salad bowl.
2. Toss to coat everything.
3. Serve.

Nutrition Info:

- Per Servings 9g Carbs, 5g Protein, 15g Fat, 198 Calories

Traditional Greek Salad

Servings: 4 | Cooking Time: 10 Minutes

Ingredients:

- 5 tomatoes, chopped
- 1 large cucumber, chopped
- 1 green bell pepper, chopped
- 1 small red onion, chopped
- 16 kalamata olives, chopped
- 4 tbsp capers
- 1 cup feta cheese, chopped
- 1 tsp oregano, dried
- 4 tbsp olive oil
- Salt to taste

Directions:

1. Place tomatoes, bell pepper, cucumber, onion, feta cheese and olives in a bowl; mix to combine well. Season with salt. Combine capers, olive oil, and oregano, in a small bowl. Drizzle with the dressing to serve.

Nutrition Info:

- Per Servings 8g Carbs, 9.3g Protein, 28g Fat, 323 Calories

Sour Cream And Cucumbers

Servings: 8 | Cooking Time: 0 Minutes

Ingredients:

- ½ cup sour cream
- 3 tablespoons white vinegar
- 4 medium cucumbers, sliced thinly
- 1 small sweet onion, sliced thinly
- Salt and pepper to taste
- 3 tablespoons olive oil

Directions:

1. In a bowl, whisk the sour cream and vinegar. Season with salt and pepper to taste. Whisk until well-combined.
2. Add in the cucumber and the rest of the ingredients.
3. Toss to coat.
4. Allow chilling before serving.

Nutrition Info:

- Per Servings 4.8g Carbs, 0.9g Protein, 8.3g Fat, 96 Calories

Salsa Verde Chicken Soup

Servings: 4 | Cooking Time: 15 Minutes

Ingredients:

- ½ cup salsa verde
- 2 cups cooked and shredded chicken
- 2 cups chicken broth
- 1 cup shredded cheddar cheese
- 4 ounces cream cheese
- ½ tsp chili powder
- ½ tsp ground cumin
- ½ tsp fresh cilantro, chopped
- Salt and black pepper, to taste

Directions:

1. Combine the cream cheese, salsa verde, and broth, in a food processor; pulse until smooth. Transfer the mixture to a pot and place over medium heat. Cook until hot, but do not bring to a boil.
2. Add chicken, chili powder, and cumin and cook for about 3-5 minutes, or until it is heated through.
3. Stir in Cheddar cheese and season with salt and pepper to taste. If it is very thick, add a few tablespoons of water and boil for 1-3 more minutes. Serve hot in bowls sprinkled with fresh cilantro.

Nutrition Info:

- Per Servings 3g Carbs, 25g Protein, 23g Fat, 346 Calories

Slow Cooker Beer Soup With Cheddar & Sausage

Servings: 8 | Cooking Time: 8 Hr

Ingredients:

- 1 cup heavy cream
- 10 ounces sausages, sliced
- 1 cup celery, chopped
- 1 cup carrots, chopped
- 4 garlic cloves, minced
- 8 ounces cream cheese
- 1 tsp red pepper flakes
- 6 ounces beer
- 16 ounces beef stock
- 1 onion, diced
- 1 cup cheddar cheese, grated
- Salt and black pepper, to taste
- Fresh cilantro, chopped, to garnish

Directions:

1. Turn on the slow cooker. Add beef stock, beer, sausages, carrots, onion, garlic, celery, salt, red pepper flakes, and black pepper, and stir to combine. Pour in enough water to cover all the ingredients by roughly 2 inches. Close the lid and cook for 6 hours on Low.
2. Open the lid and stir in the heavy cream, cheddar, and cream cheese, and cook for 2 more hours. Ladle the soup into bowls and garnish with cilantro before serving. Yummy!

Nutrition Info:

- Per Servings 4g Carbs, 5g Protein, 17g Fat, 244 Calories

Tuna Caprese Salad

Servings: 4 | Cooking Time: 10 Minutes

Ingredients:

- 2 cans tuna chunks in water, drained
- 2 tomatoes, sliced
- 8 oz fresh mozzarella cheese, sliced
- 6 basil leaves
- ½ cup black olives, pitted and sliced
- 2 tbsp extra virgin olive oil
- ½ lemon, juiced

Directions:

1. Place the tuna in the center of a serving platter. Arrange the cheese and tomato slices around the tuna. Alternate a slice of tomato, cheese, and a basil leaf.
2. To finish, scatter the black olives over the top, drizzle with olive oil and lemon juice, and serve with grilled chicken breasts.

Nutrition Info:

- Per Servings 1g Carbs, 21g Protein, 31g Fat, 360 Calories

Clam Chowder

Servings: 5 | Cooking Time: 10 Minutes

Ingredients:

- 1 can condensed cream of celery soup, undiluted
- 2 cups half-and-half cream
- 2 cans minced/chopped clams, drained
- 1/4 teaspoon ground nutmeg
- 5 tablespoons butter
- Pepper to taste

Directions:

1. In a large saucepan, combine all ingredients. Cook and stir over medium heat until heated through.

Nutrition Info:

- Per Servings 3.8g Carbs, 10g Protein, 14g Fat, 251 Calories

Coconut, Green Beans, And Shrimp Curry Soup

Servings: 4 | Cooking Time: 20 Minutes

Ingredients:

- 2 tbsp ghee
- 1 lb jumbo shrimp, peeled and deveined
- 2 tsp ginger-garlic puree
- 2 tbsp red curry paste
- 6 oz coconut milk
- Salt and chili pepper to taste
- 1 bunch green beans, halved

Directions:

1. Melt ghee in a medium saucepan over medium heat. Add the shrimp, season with salt and pepper, and cook until they are opaque, 2 to 3 minutes. Remove shrimp to a plate. Add the ginger-garlic puree and red curry paste to the ghee and sauté for 2 minutes until fragrant.
2. Stir in the coconut milk; add the shrimp, salt, chili pepper, and green beans. Cook for 4 minutes. Reduce the heat to a simmer and cook an additional 3 minutes, occasionally stirring. Adjust taste with salt, fetch soup into serving bowls, and serve with cauli rice.

Nutrition Info:

- Per Servings 2g Carbs, 9g Protein, 35.4g Fat, 375 Calories

Bacon And Pea Salad

Servings: 6 | Cooking Time: 5 Minutes

Ingredients:
- 4 bacon strips
- 2 cups fresh peas
- ½ cup shredded cheddar cheese
- ½ cup ranch salad dressing
- 1/3 cup chopped red onions
- Salt and pepper to taste
- 3 tablespoons olive oil

Directions:

1. Heat skillet over medium flame and fry the bacon until crispy or until the fat has rendered. Transfer into a plate lined with a paper towel and crumble.
2. In a bowl, combine the rest of the ingredients and toss to coat.
3. Add in the bacon bits last.

Nutrition Info:
- Per Servings 2.9g Carbs, 3.5g Protein, 20.4g Fat, 205 Calories

Lobster Salad With Mayo Dressing

Servings: 4 | Cooking Time: 1 Hour 10 Minutes

Ingredients:
- 1 small head cauliflower, cut into florets
- ⅓ cup diced celery
- ½ cup sliced black olives
- 2 cups cooked large shrimp
- 1 tbsp dill, chopped
- Dressing:
- ½ cup mayonnaise
- 1 tsp apple cider vinegar
- ¼ tsp celery seeds
- A pinch of black pepper
- 2 tbsp lemon juice
- 2 tsp swerve
- Salt to taste

Directions:

1. Combine the cauliflower, celery, shrimp, and dill in a large bowl. Whisk together the mayonnaise, vinegar, celery seeds, black pepper, sweetener, and lemon juice in another bowl. Season with salt to taste.
2. Pour the dressing over and gently toss to combine; refrigerate for 1 hour. Top with olives to serve.

Nutrition Info:
- Per Servings 2g Carbs, 12g Protein, 15g Fat, 182 Calories

Week 1

	Breakfast	Lunch	Dinner
Day 1	Lemony Fried Artichokes 14	Habanero And Beef Balls 37	Chicken Cabbage Soup 85
Day 2	Parmesan Crackers 14	Shrimp And Cauliflower Jambalaya 56	Asparagus Niçoise Salad 86
Day 3	Spicy Chicken Cucumber Bites 15	Moroccan Style Beef Stew 37	Arugula Prawn Salad With Mayo Dressing 86
Day 4	Cobb Salad With Blue Cheese Dressing 15	Steamed Ginger Scallion Fish 56	Rustic Beef Soup 86
Day 5	Bacon Jalapeno Poppers 16	Pancetta Sausage With Kale 38	Tuna Salad With Lettuce & Olives 87
Day 6	Ricotta And Pomegranate 16	Lemon Marinated Salmon With Spices 55	Green Salad 87
Day 7	Choco And Coconut Bars 16	Mustardy Pork Chops 39	Brussels Sprouts Salad With Pecorino Romano 88

Week 2

	Breakfast	Lunch	Dinner
Day 1	Balsamic Zucchini 17	Baked Calamari And Shrimp 55	Chicken And Cauliflower Rice Soup 88
Day 2	Crispy Keto Pork Bites 17	Cherry-balsamic Sauced Beef 39	Mediterranean Salad 89
Day 3	Easy Garlic Keto Bread 18	Baked Salmon With Pistachio Crust 54	Chicken Creamy Soup 89
Day 4	Devilled Eggs With Sriracha Mayo 18	Sweet Chipotle Grilled Ribs 39	Green Mackerel Salad 89
Day 5	Cheesy Chicken Fritters With Dill Dip 19	Cedar Salmon With Green Onion 54	Insalata Caprese 90
Day 6	Apricot And Soy Nut Trail Mix 20	Bacon Stew With Cauliflower 40	Thyme & Wild Mushroom Soup 90
Day 7	Cheesy Green Bean Crisps 20	Avocado & Cauliflower Salad With Prawns 54	Traditional Greek Salad 91

Week 3

	Breakfast	Lunch	Dinner
Day 1	Tofu Stuffed Peppers 21	Seasoned Salmon With Parmesan 53	Coconut Cauliflower Soup 90
Day 2	Crispy Chorizo With Cheesy Topping 20	Jalapeno Beef Pot Roasted 40	Kale And Brussels Sprouts 91
Day 3	Keto-approved Trail Mix 21	Mustard-crusted Salmon 53	Sour Cream And Cucumbers 91
Day 4	Balsamic Brussels Sprouts With Prosciutto 22	Classic Meatloaf 40	Salsa Verde Chicken Soup 92
Day 5	Sausage Roll 64	Steamed Greek Snapper 52	Slow Cooker Beer Soup With Cheddar & Sausage 92
Day 6	Morning Granola 63	Pork Burgers With Caramelized Onion Rings 41	Tuna Caprese Salad 93
Day 7	Tofu Sandwich With Cabbage Slaw 63	Red Curry Halibut 52	Clam Chowder 93

Week 4

	Breakfast	Lunch	Dinner
Day 1	Mint Chocolate Protein Shake 75	North African Lamb 41	Coconut, Green Beans, And Shrimp Curry Soup 93
Day 2	Coconut Bars 75	Simply Steamed Alaskan Cod 51	Bacon And Pea Salad 94
Day 3	Lemony-avocado Cilantro Shake 75	Greek Pork With Olives 42	Lobster Salad With Mayo Dressing 94
Day 4	Raspberry-choco Shake 76	Yummy Shrimp Fried Rice 50	Coconut Cheesecake 78
Day 5	Walnut Cookies 77	Mushroom & Jalapeño Stew 66	Bell Pepper Stuffed Avocado 62
Day 6	Nutty Choco Milk Shake 77	Air Fryer Seasoned Salmon Fillets 50	Zucchini Noodles 64
Day 7	Eggnog Keto Custard 77	Greek Styled Veggie-rice 65	Pumpkin Bake 65

A

B

Black Olives
Lemon Grilled Veggie 68

Blue Cheese
Cobb Salad With Blue Cheese Dressing 15

Blueberry
Morning Coconut Smoothie 72

Broccoli
Colorful Vegan Soup 73

Brussels Sprout
Brussels Sprouts Salad With Pecorino Romano 88
Kale And Brussels Sprouts 91
Balsamic Brussels Sprouts With Prosciutto 22

Bun
Vegetarian Burgers 70

C

Cabbage
Asian-style Fish Salad 51
Parmesan Roasted Cabbage 68
Chicken Cabbage Soup 85

Cashew
Raspberry Nut Truffles 79

Cauliflower
Shrimp And Cauliflower Jambalaya 56
Mushroom & Cauliflower Bake 62
Greek Styled Veggie-rice 65
Spicy Cauliflower Steaks With Steamed Green Beans 69
Grilled Cauliflower 71
Cauliflower & Hazelnut Salad 71
Coconut Cauliflower Soup 90
Lobster Salad With Mayo Dressing 94

Cauliflower Rice
Chicken And Cauliflower Rice Soup 88

Cheddar Cheese
Chicken And Green Cabbage Casserole 32

Cheese
White Chocolate Cheesecake Bites 81

Chicken
Spicy Chicken Cucumber Bites 15
Rotisserie Chicken With Garlic Paprika 27
Roasted Chicken With Herbs 35
Chicken Creamy Soup 89
Salsa Verde Chicken Soup 92

Chicken Breast

Cheesy Chicken Fritters With Dill Dip 19
Pacific Chicken 25
Pesto Chicken 25
Chicken And Mushrooms 26
Quattro Formaggi Chicken 28
Baked Pecorino Toscano Chicken 28
Spinach & Ricotta Stuffed Chicken Breasts 29
Red Wine Chicken 29
Sweet Garlic Chicken Skewers 30
Chicken Breasts With Walnut Crust 31
Easy Creamy Chicken 31
Cilantro Chicken Breasts With Mayo-avocado Sauce 33
Fried Chicken Breasts 34
Chicken And Spinach 34
Chicken Jambalaya 35

Chicken Thighs

Chicken, Eggplant And Gruyere Gratin 27
One-pot Chicken With Mushrooms And Spinach 30
Paprika Chicken With Cream Sauce 41

Chicken Wing

Air Fryer Garlic Chicken Wings 19
Habanero Chicken Wings 33
Sticky Cranberry Chicken Wings 34

Chorizo

Crispy Chorizo With Cheesy Topping 20

Coconut

Choco And Coconut Bars 16
Coconut Raspberry Bars 81

Coconut Milk

Coconut Bars 75
Coconut Fat Bombs 80
Cardamom-cinnamon Spiced Coco-latte 83

Cod

Simply Steamed Alaskan Cod 51
Cod In Garlic Butter Sauce 52
Baked Codfish With Lemon 58

Cream

Clam Chowder 93

Cucumber

Sour Cream And Cucumbers 91

K

L

M

P

Pork Casserole 48

Pork Belly
Crispy Keto Pork Bites 17

Pork Chop
Greek Pork With Olives 42
Creamy Pork Chops 47

Pork Loin Chop
Mustardy Pork Chops 39

Pork Sausage
Pancetta Sausage With Kale 38

Prawn
Avocado & Cauliflower Salad With Prawns 54
Arugula Prawn Salad With Mayo Dressing 86

Pumpkin
Pumpkin Bake 65

Pumpkin Seed
Apricot And Soy Nut Trail Mix 20

R

Raspberry
Raspberry-choco Shake 76

Ricotta Cheese
Ricotta And Pomegranate 16

S

Salad Green
Green Mackerel Salad 89

Salmon
Air Fryer Seasoned Salmon Fillets 50
Mustard-crusted Salmon 53
Seasoned Salmon With Parmesan 53
Cedar Salmon With Green Onion 54
Baked Salmon With Pistachio Crust 54
Lemon Marinated Salmon With Spices 55

Shrimp
Yummy Shrimp Fried Rice 50
Baked Calamari And Shrimp 55
Shrimp Stuffed Zucchini 57
Angel Hair Shirataki With Creamy Shrimp 58
Lemon Garlic Shrimp 59
Bang Bang Shrimps 60

Printed in Great Britain
by Amazon